The Magic of
JAPAN

Secret Places and Life-changing Experiences

HÉCTOR GARCÍA

TUTTLE Publishing
Tokyo | Rutland, Vermont | Singapore

"True poetry consists of leading a beautiful life. To live poetry is better than to write it."

—Matsuo Basho

INTRODUCTION

My Fifteen Years in Japan

It seems like yesterday I landed in Japan for the first time, but it's already been a decade and a half. I was twenty-three when I arrived and ready to devour the world like some wild, fearless cat; now I'm thirty-eight and I look at the world more from the perspective of a bird, observing and analyzing.

Many years have passed, but the burning curiosity that makes me want to understand and continue to explore the culture of this country hasn't diminished in the slightest.

When I arrived in Japan I experienced culture shock as I confronted a society was unfamiliar to me, but now I feel like any other resident of Tokyo. I'm at ease here and I know more or less how things work; you could say that I live within my comfort zone. Now I feel a shock when I get on a plane and travel to other countries and have to deal with non-Japanese cultures.

Japan has become my home. Every time I land at Tokyo's Haneda or Narita Airport, I feel I'm back in the place where my heart belongs.

The first few years as a foreigner here remind you of being a child again, a time when you were encountering life for the first time and couldn't stop asking questions of your parents. Everything is new and exciting; you get the feeling you're exploring a distant planet populated by strange beings. Walking through the streets you can't read even half the signs and notices; your brain is in a

As well as visiting the Ghibli Museum several times, I've also been lucky enough to visit the offices where Hayao Miyazaki and the Studio Ghibli artists work.

constant state of activity as you try to make sense of this new world.

Everything you come across grabs your attention, from your first magical and unforgettable sighting of Mount Fuji, down to the yellow lines on the sidewalks and the station platforms. If you're a photographer or a designer, the stimulus to your creativity is exhilarating.

There's so much detail, both in the urban landscape and in the countryside, that at first it takes you by surprise and it can be hard to take everything in. What's magical is that feeling of being transported to another dimension.

I'm certain that it's all this newness and unfamiliarity that is so stimulating and seductive for those who've just arrived, and is one of the main reasons why Japan is such an attractive and addictive place to visit — if people travel to Japan once, they're highly likely to come back again.

But eventually, if you settle here, once you get to grips with the language and adapt to your new surroundings, everything gradually becomes more normal and you start to feel like one of the locals. When you've seen Mount Fuji hundreds of times you realize it's always there on the horizon, keeping watch over Tokyo, a regular feature of everyday life.

When that first thrilling stage of being the new

The sculpture *Yellow Pumpkin* (1994) by Yayoi Kusama, on the island of Naoshima, has become one of Japan's magical landmarks.

arrival has passed and you want to feel more accepted by society — to be treated like just another member of staff in a Japanese company, for example — that's when you might come up against certain immovable obstacles. I don't use the word "immovable" lightly: I've discovered that appearances can be deceptive and what may seem at first sight to be a very friendly society, is true only superficially and in context.

I've been coming up against closed doors in Japan for years, and have rarely succeeded in opening them. I'm not alone; foreigners who've been here for years have realized that you have to accept the role of *gaijin* ("foreigner," lit., "person from the outside.")

The United States is an example of a more integrationist culture: you can arrive as a foreigner and over the years you can actually become another American. Whereas here nobody will ever call me "Japanese." But I'm not complaining; I've reached the conclusion that it's better that way, because I will always want to be myself.

"I'm turning Japanese" sang pop group the Vapors in 1980, and you may well feel that way when you first arrive in Japan and you're still exploring the place with an open heart. But I've never turned Japanese in the way the song says, and that's a good thing, because I'm still me, with my own identity, although I'm not the same man I was fifteen years ago. I have to thank this place and its people for having turned me into the person I am now.

Japan fits my personality very well, because I'm not someone who wants to put down roots anywhere. I don't want to be categorized as someone who comes from a certain place, I simply want to be an inhabitant of planet Earth. In this sense Japan is the ideal place for me since I'll always be a "person from the outside."

My home is where my heart is. The physical location of that home is less and less important to me. I'm as happy when I travel as when I come back to Tokyo.

神は細部に宿る
God Is in the Details

As the saying goes in English, "the devil is in the details." There's a similar saying in Japanese, but the connotation is more positive: "gods/spirits are in the details," whose translation I have broken down below. I hesitate when it comes to translating the first word **kami** 神, because the concept of "god" for Japanese people is very different to the Western concept (see chapter 6). The reputation the Japanese have for attention to detail is real at all levels: whether it's the organization of a city's streets, product design or human relationships—if you're a customer in a store, for example, you'll find yourself treated like royalty.

神は細部細部宿る **kami wa saibu ni yadoru**

神 **kami** *god or spirit*

は **wa** *particle*

細部 **saibu** *details*

に **ni** *particle*

宿る **yadoru** *to dwell*

Of course, I miss my family and my friends. My heart feels torn when I have to choose, but my home is no longer a fixed point for the rest of my life; it travels with me wherever I go.

A Third of My Life in Japan

I arrived in Japan when I was twenty-three, with three hundred euros in my pocket and one suitcase containing some clothes, a few books, and a two-megapixel camera. For the first few months I stayed in an apartment measuring six tatami mats — about a hundred square feet (ten square meters). I'd recently finished my university studies and I had a whole new world before me to discover. Having nothing to lose I thought I was invincible, but at the same time I felt quite lonely; I was surrounded by millions of people, but they were all strangers.

Over the years I've made good friends, traveled throughout Japan and other Asian countries finding new and interesting places. I've met

Colors, lines, order and the little details let us know we're in Japan.

extraordinary people and worked in several leading technology companies — one of my most thrilling experiences was to be part of the pioneering group that brought Twitter to Japan.

But what has added a special touch to my life here are certain anecdotal events, moments I would describe as surreal because when I recall them I have the feeling that maybe they never happened.

My friend Rodrigo, who's also been in Tokyo for more than a decade, is always saying to me: "You have to invest in stories."

Some of the best moments from my collection of stories have been my appearances on Japanese television. On a TV program shown by Japan's public broadcaster NHK, I had to eat snake meat in front of the camera and give my opinion on how it tasted. On a show broadcast by the network Fuji TV, I had to play the role of tourist guide around a Tokyo neighborhood for a famous Japanese television personality, taking him to my favorite places.

Which is more beautiful, the reflection or reality? Which is more real? If you live inside the reflection perhaps you'll never know what's beyond, and vice versa. I took this photo on one of my trips to Kyoto's Temple of the Golden Pavilion.

On Tokyo MX news, the newsreader held up my first book, *A Geek in Japan*, and explained that it was the bestselling book abroad about Japan.

Something else that I can hardly believe happened was when one of Japan's most famous theater directors chose a photo from one of my trips to use on the tickets and flyers for his latest work when it was opening at the National Theater of Japan.

An interesting period of my life began thanks to a collaboration with the Massachusetts Institute of Technology research laboratory, MIT Media Lab, when I ended up renting a rice-growing plot in Chiba Prefecture to test a system to monitor rice production using IoT devices.

Through a work project, I also had the chance to

meet and have dinner with Masi Oka, the actor who played the legendary character Hiro Nakamura in America's NBC television series *Heroes*.

Many years ago I tried to pursue my dream of working in the video game industry. I had several interviews with Nintendo which seemed to go well, and got as far as what I was told would be the final interview in front of several company executives, where they decided I wasn't the right person for the job.

Eventually I abandoned my childhood ambition of working in games production. But I still remember the Nintendo interviews and I have a story about a couple of badly paid afternoons of work in which I had the honor of voicing one of the characters from the game *Ace Attorney* (Gyakuten saiban) for Nintendo DS.

I also had the opportunity to meet Dr Nakamatsu, the person with the highest ever number of patents to his name, even more than Thomas Edison. He met me at his Tokyo mansion and explained his creative process in great detail.

Another extraordinary experience that's close

芸能人 Geinojin

A **geinojin** 芸能人, also known as a **talento** タレント, is a famous personality who often appears on television. Some geinojin start off appearing on TV variety shows, and thanks to that end up becoming well known. Others are people with real talent, such as actors and singers.

One of the largest groups of **geinojin** are comedians, of which there are thousands in Japan. In order to be considered a **geinojin**, you normally have to be signed to an agency, which takes responsibility for nominating you to appear in television programs or at other events.

The literal translation of **geinojin** could be "person with talent," where the meaning of each character is as follows:

芸 **gei** *art*
能 **no** *skill, talent, ability*
人 **jin** *person*

BELOW LEFT The Appearance of my first book, *A Geek in Japan*, on Japanese TV news.

ABOVE RIGHT I spent a day with Dr. Nakamatsu, the most famous Japanese inventor.

外国人・外人
Gaikokujin or Gaijin?

The word **gaikokujin**, or **gaijin** for short, is used to mean foreigner in the Japanese language. The longer version of the word, **gaikokujin**, is more formal, whereas **gaijin** is used in casual situations.

Gaijin is written 外人. The first character 外 means "outside" and the second character 人 means "person." **Gaikokujin** is written 外国人: the first and last characters are the same as those of **gaijin**, and the middle character 国 means "country" or "region."

to my heart was meeting Hayao Miyazaki and Toshio Suzuki, founders of Studio Ghibli, my favorite maker of animated movies.

Since the day I first landed at Narita Airport I've written about my experiences on a blog at kirainet.com and over the years I've published seven books analyzing different aspects of Japan; the one you're holding is number eight.

Anyone who lives here in Japan, especially in Tokyo, is exposed to a huge number of opportunities if he or she is prepared to move around and look for them.

But life hasn't always been a bed of roses for me since I came here.

That's me in the picture, playing music and dancing games with geisha in Niigata. The geisha of Niigata are known as *furumachi geigi.*

The shallow waters of the Katsura River in Kyoto reflect the green of the surrounding forest, giving the scene a beautiful aura.

I started up a business with a partner and it fell through. Losing the money I'd saved during my first few years in Japan and having to start again from scratch wasn't easy.

As an employee I've also had my low points; in one of the companies I worked for things went badly wrong and I was fired, Japanese style. In chapter 7, I'll tell you what happened in detail.

But these are mere trifles compared with the hardest thing by far, namely fighting a chronic intestinal illness called SIBO which attacks me relentlessly every day. I've been suffering with it for years, and having to deal with the medical system here isn't easy.

Another miserable time was living through the earthquake, tsunami and nuclear disaster in 2011 at close quarters. I was in a skyscraper when the earthquake struck and although I was frightened at the time, with hindsight I was never in any immi-nent danger, being relatively far removed from the earthquake's epicenter and subsequent tsunami. Even so, the dozens of daily aftershocks in Tokyo,

and the continuous threat of possible nuclear contamination from the nearby Fukushima plant was enough to put all the city's inhabitants into an intense state of anxiety and fear. Later on, I had the chance to visit the Miyagi and Fukushima coastal towns that had been ravaged by the tsunami; I'll tell you all about it in chapter 9.

But let's put the difficult stories to one side and get back to the good, the positive and the beautiful!

Perhaps my most magical experience was my wedding, at a Shinto shrine by the ocean in Oki-nawa. The moment when my wife and I addressed the *kami* (gods or spirits) directly, with nobody there to come between us and them, is forever engraved in my heart.

I keep peeling back the thousands of layers of the onion skin which make up this culture. In my first book *A Geek In Japan*, I shared with readers my observations and reflections on Japanese society. In this new book we'll go deeper, to try to reach the heart of the onion.

Good or not so good, I love this land. Everything I write is a tribute to this place and to the people who live in it.

"What makes you want to stay in Japan?" is one of the questions I've been asked most over recent years. It's not an easy question to answer; I could respond with objective facts, saying that I work here or that I married a Japanese woman. But that's not enough, because I could go somewhere else with my wife and find a new job; I sense that the truth about why I'm still here goes deeper.

Little by little I've reached the conclusion that what keeps me here is the mystery and magic of Japan. To this I'd have to add my endless curiosity as I strive to get to know the soul of this country.

My *ikigai* (reason for being) is to give into my curiosity, to write about what I learn and to communicate it to others. Why do I use the word "magic" and not a different word? Because even when I think that I've found explanations for every Japanese cultural phenomenon, I often end up realizing that things weren't what they seemed and that I was wrong. Suddenly my perspective changes, as though I've been taken in by a magic trick — I thought I knew how it was done, but then I realize that I actually knew nothing.

So, the definitive answer to the question "What makes you stay here?" is: *the magic of Japan*.

Dear readers, together let's explore the key concepts that have shaped the Japanese mentality, philosophy and way of life, and discover what it is that has made Japanese culture so unique and magical.

Welcome to the endless mystery
and magic of Japan!

—Héctor, Tokyo 2021

The magic and mystery hidden in each of the layers of the onion of this culture is one of the key factors which captivates my curiosity and compels me to stay.

"How strange it is to be alive beneath the sakura!"

—Kobayashi Issa

CHAPTER 1
The Magic of Japan

There's something magical in each of the cultures that inhabit this planet. It's our mission as human beings to care for and to appreciate each one; they all have something unique and distinctive. Of course there are also things everywhere that we find unpleasant, but for the moment let's concentrate on the good, the beautiful and the magical.

I like to analyze cultures through the analogy of the fish. The sea represents the culture in which we live and we human beings are the fish that live in this sea. If you're a fish that has spent its whole life in the depths of the sea, perhaps you end up thinking that you know everything there is to know about it. But what happens if one day you jump out of the water and you see the sea from the outside? You may suffer a kind of shock.

Just like the fish that realizes the sea it's been swimming in all its life doesn't constitute the entire universe, the same thing happens to us humans when we spend many years stuck in the same surroundings and then suddenly we travel, or we go to live in a faraway place.

Being in Japan I have learned about its culture, and this in turn has helped me to appreciate my own culture in a different way, not from within the sea, but from without. Of course, after so many years here, I'm beginning to feel

like a Japanese fish, and now I feel a certain culture shock when I travel back to Spain.

When you live for a time in one place, it starts to become familiar and many of the things that caught your attention at the beginning gradually stop surprising you and start to become part of everyday life.

But it's not the sea that stops being beautiful and exciting, it is we fish who lose the sensitivity with which to admire it. This is what is happening to me after so long here; if I don't make the effort, every-

LEFT A traditional Japanese dancer at my wedding.
RIGHT A woman lights incense at Kiyomizu-dera temple. Incense is one of the elements that tells us we are at a Buddhist temple (not at a Shinto shrine).

thing starts to seem "normal." To combat the apathy of habit, I use my love of photography.

Taking photos helps me focus on the things that feed my curiosity every day and trains my eye to pick out what is special or magical about Japan.

For me, magic is something that has an ingredient that can be explained but also an ingredient that is inexplicable: something surprising or mysterious. For example, good art is capable of generating magic, because no matter how much you try to explain or understand it, there is always something in it that can only be felt. Magic means you never really know what to expect. It's like a novel that's interesting from start to finish because you're always wondering what's going to happen next, with the exhilaration of the explorer.

The uncertainty we feel when we travel to a place we don't know has the power to activate the human capacity to perceive beauty and magic.

Mr. Casca and Ms. Wonder

There are many kinds of traveler, but in general I would divide them into two main categories: the

The magic of Japan can be felt by the sensitive traveler, especially at a shrine or temple that is surrounded by nature.

person with an inflated ego who thinks that his own life is better than what he sees when he travels, and the person who has had so many experiences that she knows there's something good, something bad and something beautiful in every place and culture on the planet.

I'm going to create two fictional characters that I will use throughout this book:

Mr. Casca (from the Spanish word *cascarrabias*, meaning "grouch") is a man of fifty years of age who, although he has traveled widely, is always convinced that the food from his home town is the best, and that his friend Pepe is the best site supervisor on the planet. Walking through Osaka, every fourth street he complains of how badly built everything is and he loves to explain to his wife how his friend Pepe would do it better. The truth is that Mr. Casca isn't really interested in traveling: what he wants is always to be right and to be able to impose his views wherever he goes. What he thinks is true is absolutely and unshakably true.

Ms. Wonder, when she comes across something she can't understand or someone behaving strangely, is curious, and finds herself asking questions to try to understand. Ms. Wonder knows that no matter how much you learn about the things you encounter while you're traveling, the truth will always be partial and will depend on the lens through which things are seen, and that's exactly where the interesting part of traveling lies. When Ms. Wonder goes back to her home town after traveling she always feels changed, a different person, and she also sees her own town and its people in a more special way. Ms. Wonder is capable of seeing magic more than most.

The last time I was in Kyoto I revisited the temple of Kizomizu-dera. Erected on the side of a mountain to the east of Kyoto, with views of the city and surrounded by forest, it's one of the most spectacular Buddhist temples in the country. The wooden columns that support it are majestic and they manage to create the sensation that the whole complex is floating above the forest, keeping watch over the city.

I was there at dusk and the sunlight tinged the wood with ochre tones. The floorboards reflected the shadows of the tourists in a strange way, giving the sensation that they, the shadows, were living beings. A girl dressed in a *yukata* summer kimono stopped for a while to light incense; the smoke and the aroma added an even more magical touch to the sunset.

You could hear the murmur of visitors talking discreetly, birdsong in the trees and little else. But all of a sudden the peace was shattered by a voice, almost shouting, saying in Spanish: "Look at the state of these columns! We've come half way round the world to see an old building that's rotting to pieces."

I blinked, trying to ignore what I'd just heard. But he carried on.

"This building has no architectural value," he said to his partner as if he were lecturing on the subject. Finally, the last thing I remember him saying was: "Let's hope that woman gets out of the way now, so I can take this photograph and we can get out of here." It wasn't a pleasant experience bumping into someone like this, but I have to thank this man because it was he who inspired the creation of the character Mr. Casca that I will be using in this book.

He also helped me to reflect a little, because in a slightly less exaggerated way I too have been a bit Mr. Casca on occasion. I suspect that we all have. So that we don't fall into the ego trap of thinking that what we have is always best, the trick is to catch yourself when you're thinking like Mr. Casca and to change your attitude: instead of projecting your beliefs onto what you're looking at, try asking yourself questions so that you can understand the history of what you're looking at from the perspective of the local people.

Standing before this *torii* gate Mr. Casca would say: "Have I come all the way to Japan to look at four pieces of wood? What a disappointment." By contrast Ms. Wonder would say: "I'm fascinated by the simplicity of Shinto shrines, there's something that makes me feel different when I walk through one of these gates."

清水の舞台から飛び降りる
To Jump from the Platform of Kiyomizu-dera Temple

There is a popular saying in the Japanese language, "to jump from the platform of Kiyomizu-dera temple." It's been used for hundreds of years to refer to the risk of confronting the unknown. A non-literal translation could be "to take a decisive step" or "to take a leap of faith in the darkness."

Now it is merely an expression, but in the past it was actually done. People would go to Kyoto to jump from the temple platform, because it was believed that if you survived, all your wishes would be granted. During the Edo period (1603–1868), 234 people jumped and 199 of them survived. It's a 42 foot (13 meter) jump and there are trees below.

Today the jump is prohibited. But there is a much easier way to make your wishes. Near the base of the platform from which people used to jump, water pours from the mountainside in three separate streams. It is believed that drinking this water will make your dreams come true.

In Japanese the expression is 清水の舞台から飛び降りる **Kiyomizu no butai kara tobioriru:**

清水 **Kiyomizu** is the temple name without the suffix "dera" meaning temple. Kizomizu literally means, "pure, crystalline water"

の **no** *of*

舞台 **butai** *platform* (or theater stage)

から **kara** *from*

飛び降りる **tobioriru**, *to jump off*

FACING PAGE, TOP Kiyomizu-dera temple.
FACING PAGE, BOTTOM Schoolboys drink the water that has
the power to make all your dreams come true.

ABOVE When you walk down the narrow Shinjuku alley
Omoide Yokocho (lit., Memory Lane), you'll feel as though
you've been transported fifty years into the past.

MY TRAVEL TIPS
Visiting Kiyomizu-dera

As a UNESCO World Heritage Site, Kiyomizu-dera temple is
often crowded with tourists and Japanese visitors. To avoid
the crowds, don't go on weekends. If you're an early riser,
the temple is open from six in the morning. You don't need
to get there so early to enjoy the temple, but there is a big
difference between the experience of walking around the
monument at eight in the morning when there are almost
no people, and at ten in the morning when the hordes of
tourists have arrived.

The temple closes at six, and if you go there at four or five
o'clock there are usually fewer people and you can enjoy
the sunset with unforgettable views.

From mid-November to the beginning of December there is
a special timetable which allows you to see the temple
illuminated, and the woods that surround it are tinged with
the colors of autumn (known in Japanese as **koyo** 紅葉,
where 紅 means red, and 葉 means leaves). During cherry
blossom season in March, the temple is also illuminated in
the evenings.

The special illuminated evening timetable is usually from
6 p.m. to 9 p.m., but it's a good idea to consult the
homepage Kiyomizu-dera.or.jp/en/location/#OpenHours as
times change from year to year.

HOW TO GET THERE

- From Keihan Kiyomizu Gojo Station it's a twenty-five-
minute walk to the temple.

- Bus numbers 100 and 206 both pass close to Kiyomizu-
dera temple. From the Kiyomizu-michi stop it's a
fifteen-minute walk to the temple.

- Entrance fee: ¥330

Let's be travelers whose minds are open to magic. Let's be less Mr. Casca and more Ms. Wonder.

With the right attitude and my camera in hand, now I can enjoy any random corner of the streets of Tokyo. Some well-cared for plant pots in the window of a tiny house, hidden away in the district of Setagaya? A little park with a couple of flowering cherry trees? This is all I need for a wonderful afternoon.

But I wasn't always so open to new experiences. Let's take a look back at my first brush with Japanese cherry blossom.

Outdoor dining at an izakaya, one of the most popular types of local neighborhood restaurant in Japan because of their atmosphere and the variety of food available.

Sakura, the Glorious Cherry Blossom

When people ask me what the best time of year to visit Japan is, I always tend to hesitate before giving my answer.

It doesn't matter when you come; Japan always has something different to offer. Its landscapes change appearance radically according to the seasons. Traveling here in winter, when everything is covered in snow, is a completely different experience to traveling during *sakura* (cherry blossom) season when the blossom transforms the landscape in a festival of beauty.

At first, I underestimated the magic and influence of sakura on Japanese culture. When I was told that cherry blossom season was approaching, I showed hardly any interest; I thought it would be like when the almond trees flower in

桜 The Language of Cherry Blossoms

The word *sakura* 桜 on its own can be used to refer both to the tree and the flower. Here are some other key cherry blossom terms:

開花 **kaika**, where 開 means "opening" and 花 means "flower." This is the moment when the flowering of the sakura begins. Depending on the weather in a given year and on the geographical location, the date of kaika tends to vary. In several dozen cities there is a "marker" tree that is monitored every day by the Japanese Meteorological Agency to determine the exact moment of kaika in each region.

満開 **mankai**, where 満 means "full" and 開 means "opening." This is the moment when the cherry blossom is in full bloom and usually happens approximately one week after kaika.

花吹雪 **hanafubuki**, where 花 means "flower," 吹 means "blow" and 雪 means "snow." This word is used to refer to the falling of the sakura petals after mankai, an event of extreme beauty and similar to the falling of snowflakes. It is said that the average speed at which sakura petals fall is two inches (five centimeters) per second.

花見 **hanami**, where 花 means "flower" and 見 means "look." This is the act of enjoying the sakura.

MY TRAVEL TIPS
Best Times to See Sakura

According to an average calculated from the last sixty years' worth of statistics from the Japanese Meteorological Agency, March 26 is the day that marks *kaika* (when the blossoms first open) in the Tokyo area, and April 3 marks *mankai* — the day on which the cherry trees are in full bloom.

The dates below are approximate and they tend to vary depending on the weather during the preceding months: a cold winter, for example, means a later cherry blossom season. Despite this, I would dare to suggest that if you're in Tokyo during the last week of March and the first week of April you're unlikely to miss it.

- **Kyoto:** average *kaika* is March 28, average *mankai*, April 5.
- **Hiroshima:** average *kaika* is March 27, average *mankai*, April 4.
- **Fukuoka:** average *kaika* is March 25, average *mankai*, April 1.
- **Sapporo:** average *kaika* is April 30, average *mankai*, May 4.

Spain, and nothing more, something to see from a distance as you drive along some country road.

But I was totally wrong. The Japanese cherry tree isn't just found in the mountains and in the fields, you see it also in cities, parks, along urban river banks, and in temples and shrines. When it

ABOVE The flowering of the *sakura* in Nakameguro (Tokyo) is a spectacular sight.

BELOW Cherry blossom is found in cities, parks, along river banks, and in shrines and temples.

MY TRAVEL TIPS

Best Places to Photograph Sakura in Tokyo

This map is a general guide to give you an idea of the best places to photograph cherry blossom. Look for exact locations on your favorite maps app, using the names below as search terms:

① **Yoyogi Park:** one of my favorite parks. It has a small number of cherry trees near the pond with the fountain.

② **Shinjuku Gyoen:** my favorite spot, although it's always packed with people which makes the flower-viewing less enjoyable. To avoid the crowds try going first thing in the morning. The park opens at 9 a.m.

③ **Inokashira Park:** the area around the boating lake is where the most of the blossom is.

④ **Mitsuike Park:** small but it has many varieties of cherry trees with blossoms of various colors. It's near Kawasaki Station.

⑤ **Nakameguro:** sakura blooms all along the river that runs from the station in the direction of Shibuya.

⑥ **Ueno Park:** has enormous sakura trees lining the main pathways that run through the center of the park.

⑦ **Imperial Palace:** only a few sakura but there aren't many people and it's peaceful.

⑧ **Ichigaya and Yotsuya:** most of the cherry trees are in the area around the moat.

blooms, all corners of Japan are awash with the pink and white colors of its flowers.

Before I'd heard the word sakura, I learned the word *hanami*, which means "to look at the flowers," when I was invited to a hanami party. I couldn't understand why this event was important enough to have its own name and to warrant meeting up "to look at the flowers" together.

"They've invited me to look at the flowers . . . how strange . . . ," I said to myself, a little confused. "I don't need anyone to invite me to look at flowers." This bad-tempered attitude toward hanami is in line with the Mr. Casca way of thinking. In those moments I was a Mr. Casca — this whole sakura thing seemed absurd to me and my ego made me think that what I knew was better. "There are flowers in my town too, and I bet they're prettier than the sakura!"

I consider this to be a clear indication of my lack of understanding of the culture. When you catch yourself rationalizing like Mr. Casca, it's not a bad thing: we all do it when we're outside our comfort zone; the important thing is to realize what you're doing and to change your attitude. My prejudices collapsed immediately the first time I saw a cherry tree in flower. And then there was a particular moment when I saw a single sakura flower floating on a small pond. It sat up elegantly on the water giving the sensation that the reflection of its petals in the water was more real than the flower itself. Possessed by the utter beauty of the image, I couldn't help but run toward it and start taking photographs. To this day I still remember this encounter vividly.

The following day I attended the hanami I'd been invited to. I had such a good time that I've

repeated it every year, each one being a marvellous experience. Little by little I grew to understand that the whole thing about "looking at the flowers," is just an excuse to celebrate life beneath the sakura trees. Having attended dozens of hanami with friends, work colleagues and even complete strangers, I've arrived at the conclusion that the sakura flowers are nothing more than the decorations for the biggest festival and annual celebration in Japan.

In general the Japanese are discreet, even restrained, in their end-of-year and New Year celebrations. In contrast, the sakura appears as a messenger that gives everyone permission to take a break from life's obligations and to relax under the blossoming trees with friends and family, sharing food and drink.

At the moment of *mankai* (full bloom), there is

no green to be seen on the branches of the Japanese cherry tree. You can only see the white flowers and the bark.

It's also worth mentioning the majesty of the trees, some of which can reach from thirty to fifty feet (ten to fifteen meters) in height.

The significance of the sakura for Japan is supremely important. In Tokyo the blossoming usually coincides with the last week in March and the first in April. Both the school year and the tax year for businesses begin on April 1. The sakura is a kind of artificial clock that marks the start of a new beginning, one that is even more important than New Year's Day.

Hanami cherry-blossom viewing parties are just an excuse to celebrate life while eating and drinking under the trees.

The Magic of Shinto: My Okinawa Wedding

On our wedding day we woke up at five in the morning. It was an easy task for me to get dressed in the traditional *hakama* (formal kimono, trousers and overcoat), but the bride's preparation and makeup was hours of work, hence the need to get up so early.

Once I'd put on the hakama, I remember leaving the room adjacent to the shrine, where several girls were busy dressing my wife, and contemplating the dawn. The sunlight tinged the roof of the shrine where we were to be married in tones of orange, and all that could be heard was the sound of the waves and the chatter of the birds.

The shrine is called Naminoue (lit., "above the waves"), and it's one of the few Shinto shrines in Okinawa, an archipelago in the south of Japan where traditions from many cultures intermingle. The *honden* (main building of the shrine) is built on a cliff top, with a view of the sea to the west and, to the east, the jumble of buildings that make up Naha, the capital of Okinawa.

Those moments of intense anticipation that I was able to enjoy in silence as I walked through the grounds of the shrine form one of the most beautiful memories I have of that day. Once my wife emerged from the makeup room, the roller-coaster ride of celebration began. When I look back, I have the sensation that from that point onward, everything happened in fast-forward until the very end of the day.

With traditional white makeup and lips painted red as if she were a geisha, I knew it was my wife by her eyes and her smile but the rest of her seemed to have been transformed into a kind of archetype of idealized Japanese womanhood.

With my wife transformed and myself simply clothed in a hakama, we went to have our photos taken walking along the sandy beach until our families arrived.

The leader of the shrine initiated the ceremony leading us from the *torii* entrance gate to the honden, where those present sat to the right and to the left on wooden stools.

After a series of initial rituals that consisted of saying our names and cleansing the surroundings of "evil spirits," the culmination of the ceremony was when my wife and I approached the center of

A group of young men perform traditional Okinawan drumming.

the honden holding a parchment in our hands. Upon it I had written some words in ancient Japanese that I'd had to study to understand.

Turning my back on the congregation and looking toward the center of the shrine in the direction of the sea, we broke the silence by reading those words that bound our past with our future.

At the center of the shrine there was only white gravel underfoot and the blue sky above us. Staring toward that empty space, in which there was apparently nothing special, we directly addressed the *kami* (gods), or whatever it was that each of us believed in, with the words we had prepared.

The text we read from, written in ancient Japanese, has been used for thousands of years in similar ceremonies to communicate to the kami that two people are marrying each other. In other words, in a traditional Shinto wedding ceremony, it isn't the priest who marries the bride and groom, it

The moment at our Shinto shrine wedding when the priest stepped aside, we turned our backs on our families, and addressed ourselves directly to the gods.

is the bride and groom who marry each other, speaking directly to the kami.

The feeling that it was I who married my wife myself, rather than being married by a third party, has fascinated me to the present day. I felt connected not only to my wife but also to nature and to the whole universe.

It was a magical moment.

After the ceremony in the shrine, we carried on the celebrations in a hotel, with a performance of traditional Okinawan dance followed by a flamenco show. Don't ask me about this final Spanish touch — it was all my father-in-law's idea.

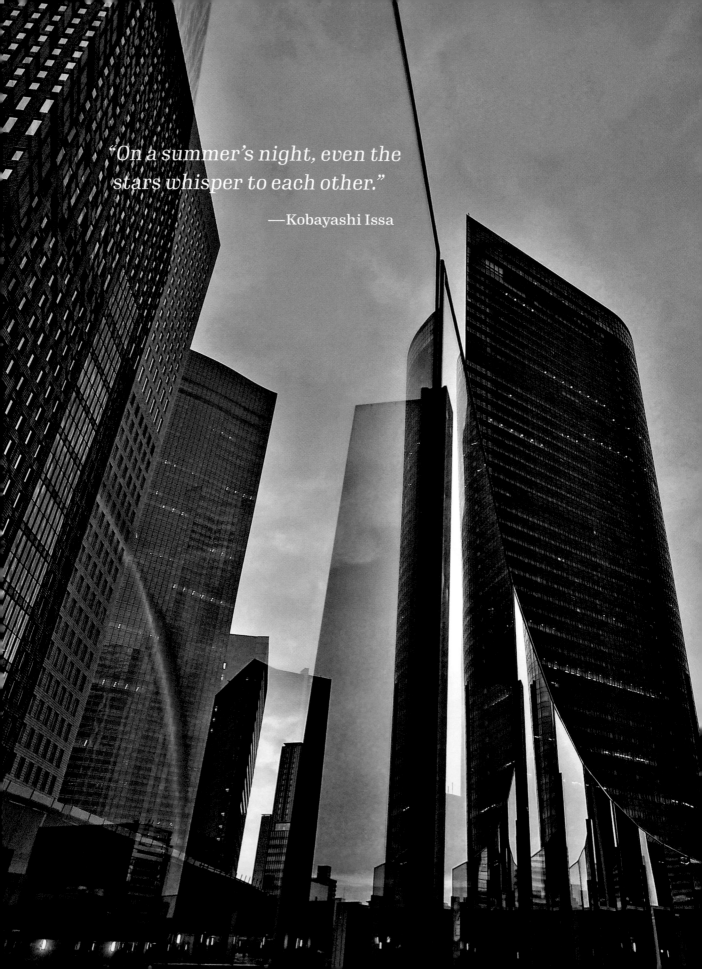

"On a summer's night, even the stars whisper to each other."

—Kobayashi Issa

CHAPTER 2

The Four Prisms of Japan

When I encounter a Japanese subject I know nothing about, I observe it from different perspectives until I arrive at a coherent initial hypothesis. But what usually happens is that if I keep turning my hypothesis around in my mind I realize my explanation is incorrect and I have to carry on analyzing it.

In fact, not even the Japanese agree on "how to explain Japan." There exists a genre of nonfiction books dedicated to this topic. This genre, called *nihonron*, is an attempt to analyze the reasons why Japan is as it is today. My previous books, *A Geek in Japan* and *Ikigai*, were translated into Japanese and they can be found in the nihonron section of bookshops in Japan.

Having read many nihonron books, I've realized that they tend to use a series of arguments that can be grouped into four main categories. Though they are subject to debate, and some may consider them clichés, they are without doubt truths which affect the Japanese psyche.

If I don't understand something, I analyze it using these four hypotheses to see what conclusions I can draw. I use them as though they were prisms through which I can observe cultural phenomena. I have decided to call these hypotheses the Four Prisms of Japan. Keep in mind that these four prisms don't always offer valid or definitive explanations, but they are useful tools that can help you form your own opinion when it comes to understanding different aspects of Japanese culture from a variety of perspectives.

A rainbow is reflected in the towering skyscrapers of Shiodome, one of Tokyo's major business districts.

The Sakoku Prism

"What are the things you like least about Japan?" my work colleague Okuda asks me one day, after we've had a few beers.

A thousand negative things come to mind, but the atmosphere is relaxed and I decide to respond with something funny:

"Well, the worst thing is it's impossible to find cheap cheese!"

They all laugh and nod their heads in agreement. I'm having dinner with several coworkers in an izakaya with a view of the moat surrounding the Imperial Palace. Our table is next to the window, the full moon is reflected in the water of the moat and the Chuo Line trains go past every few minutes.

Okuda says, "I'd really love to have cheap cheese too, but —"

"I love Spanish cheese," interrupts Takahashi, who's sitting next to the window snacking on edamame beans. "What's it called . . . Manchu . . . Manche . . ."

"Manchego!" I say.

"That's it, Manchego!"

"But it's always been this way," Okuda continues. "We have high tariffs on everything — it's this ingrained tendency we have to protect our country. In many ways we still operate as if Japan was still in *sakoku*."

"Come on, it's not that bad, when we were in

sakoku, we didn't let anything into the country at all," Takahashi retorts.

"But the mentality is the same," argues Okuda. "We block what comes from outside at all costs."

Takahashi, who's the most drunk of all of us, concludes:

"What I want is cheap Mancheeeego in the supermarkets of Tokyo. Down with tariffs!"

Sakoku was a foreign policy initiative promulgated by the Tokugawa shogunate through a series of edicts in the year 1633 banning commercial relations with almost all foreign nations. The violation of these laws, that is to say, any case of having contact with the outside world, was punishable with the death penalty.

These sakoku edicts initiated by the Tokugawa shogunate were scrapped in 1853 when Commodore Matthew Perry arrived with his US fleet on the Kanagawa coast and forced Japan to open up to the outside world.

Can you imagine how it might affect a society to be closed off from outside influence for more than two hundred years?

Between 1633 and 1853, the years of sakoku, Japan's isolation was not total, however. Some thirty foreign expeditions were permitted to land in Japan – the majority of them in the port of Nagasaki – and business with China was conducted via the Ryukyu Kingdom (what is now Okinawa). But these contacts with the exterior are little more than anecdotal; the reality is that the Japanese population lived for just over two centuries with hardly any contact with the outside world.

There are various hypotheses that attempt to explain the reason why the Tokugawa shogunate initiated sakoku:

- To minimize or eliminate the influence of other religions; the shogunate feared Christianity above all. Saint Francis Xavier (from Navarre in

The American fleet was described by the Japanese as the "Black Ships."

present-day Spain) was the first to introduce the Christian doctrine in the year 1549 when he went to Japan as a missionary. When the Tokugawa shogunate came to power half a century later, Christianity had already spread widely, especially in the south (present-day Kyushu).

- To make sure that the daimyo (feudal lords) in regions far removed from Edo (present-day Tokyo) did not become too wealthy and present a future threat to the stability and control of the Tokugawa shogunate. This had been one of the main problems in the past, especially during the Sengoku (Warring States) period (1467–1615).

- Another theory is that Japan's rulers just wanted to protect the country from the threat of pirates.

It is a long time now since Japan opened up to the world, but the sakoku mentality continues to inform the decision-making processes of the government, as for example with imported cheese, where tariffs are high to protect local produce. And this is not something which only happens at government level; the business world also tends toward protectionism.

The bay of Nagasaki was one of the few places where, under special permission, business with the outside world was allowed.

Even though the country is no longer officially closed to the outside world, which aspects of sakoku are still present today in the Japanese subconscious?

One of the first things I noticed on arriving in Japan, staring through the train window on the journey from the airport to the center of Tokyo, was the presence of tiny cube-shaped cars. Later I learned that these cars are called *kei* cars – "light-weight" cars with a maximum engine size of 660 cc – and they are very popular in Japan but not abroad. Why don't they export kei cars?

One striking effect of this way of thinking is that not only does it mean that things from the outside can't get into Japan, or only get in in a filtered way, it also means that things originating in Japan suffer from what is referred to as "Gala-pagos syndrome." In other words, many original products from Japan never see the light if day in any other part of the world – like species that are endemic to the Galapagos Islands.

Before the arrival of the global smartphone era, Japanese mobile phones suffered from Galapagos syndrome. When I arrived in 2004 one of the things which surprised me was that the mobile phones here were years ahead of the ones we had in the rest of the world. The question I continually asked myself was: why don't they sell these phones globally? The answer to this question isn't easy, but I'd say that subconsciously it has to do with sakoku.

When I asked various employees of large Japanese mobile phone companies they gave me a variety of reasons:

"The mobile phones we have here are *very Japanese,* there's no market for them abroad . . ."

"We concentrate on making the best mobile phones for Japan; there's too much competition overseas . . ."

"These mobile phones would never work in foreign markets . . ."

These answers display little optimism and a level of negativity. Selling outside Japan is not even considered as a possibility.

When you see kei cars in the streets, when you realize that elevator doors work differently from the rest of the world, when you notice everyone using their mobile phones to pay electronically for everything from subway tickets to drinks from vending machines in the middle of the countryside, when you go to a supermarket in Tokyo and you can't find more than four types of cheese, or when government protectionist policies mean you can't

Japanese mobile phones, known as *keitai*, were the precursors of smartphones, but they were never exported overseas.

Characteristics of the Sakoku Prism

- The Japanese adapt what comes from the outside to suit their own circumstances

- Japan exports more than it imports

- The Japanese take for granted that what is theirs will never work abroad, and are surprised when it does

- When something from the outside invades Japan, they attempt to adapt and modify it as much as possible and it ends up having "Japanese" characteristics

- Fear of becoming international — local firms tend to first conquer the Japanese market before moving into other markets

buy more than one packet of Japan-produced butter in the same supermarket . . .

In all these cases, whether a product is victim of Galapagos syndrome or whether it is scarce because its importation is restricted, it can be analyzed through the Sakoku Prism.

It's not something that is done maliciously, it's something that happens as a consequence of so many years of isolation and of thinking defensively when faced with things from outside.

The Prism of Natural Disasters

We don't have to visit a place to learn about its culture. Anyone who has interacted with Japanese organizations, be they public or private, will know very well how Kafkaesque the bureaucracy of business dealings in Japan can be.

Below is a list complaints and typical comments I've received over the years from people outside Japan trying to do business with the Japanese:

- They take forever to make decisions
- We've been negotiating with them for months and it's impossible for us to know if they want to move forward or not
- They go over and over the simplest of things
- Everything's going like clockwork now, but it took us forever to convince them
- They were really nice, but in the end they rejected us without even an explanation
- We share so much information but they give nothing away
- They even plan their plans — for them the important thing seems to be to plan everything, even the most trivial of things

To understand this behavior, which can be frustrating for foreigners, the best thing to do is to apply what I call the Prism of Natural Disasters.

During negotiations, we foreigners are typically thinking of the immediate economic benefits of signing a contract with the Japanese party, without thinking of what will happen more than five or ten years into the future; the Japanese side is, in all probability, considering the possible risks

HISTORY

The Great Kanto Earthquake of 1923: Will It Happen Every Hundred Years?

Around forty million people inhabit the Kanto Plain, home to Tokyo, Yokohama and Saitama and Chiba prefectures. Since I've lived in Tokyo, headlines like "Another great earthquake about to strike Kanto?" or "Ninety years have passed since the last great earthquake" recur in the media, sowing fear in the citizens.

Some say that the Kanto Plain is destined to be hit by a destructive earthquake more or less every hundred years; others say it's impossible to predict. The last one was in 1923, and it flattened more than 90 percent of the built environment of Tokyo and Yokohama.

The Spanish novelist, Vicente Blasco Ibáñez, during a round-the-world trip, arrived on the Yokohama coast just after the great earthquake. In his book *Japón* (Japan), he describes the scenes he witnessed on arrival as the nearest thing to hell that he'd seen in his life.

The miracle is that Tokyo was reborn like a phoenix, and then, barely thirty-two years later, was again reduced to rubble in World War II. Later, in the fifties and sixties, it was reborn yet again, as one of the most economically powerful cities in the world.

The Kanto region including Tokyo (above) and Yokohama (left) suffered almost total destruction after the 1923 earthquake.

ANECDOTE
Tago, the Man Who Survived Three Catastrophes

After my book *Ikigai* was translated into Japanese and published in Japan, an advertising agency contacted me. After a couple of meetings with them in their offices in Ginza, they invited me to dinner in Shinbashi.

One of the executives, whose name was Tago, seemed to be the most reserved and ate in silence for the first hour. But after a couple of beers he started to speak and tell stories about his life, which turned out to be really interesting. He'd spent more than thirty years making business trips around the world.

I don't recall how, but the theme of terrorism came up. Suddenly, Tago said to his work colleagues and to me: "I've never told you this, but I was a victim of the sarin gas attack."

The sarin gas attack was a act of domestic terrorism, carried out by a cult called Aum Shinrikyo, on the Tokyo subway in 1995. The attack killed twelve people and a further thousand were hospitalized. Tago was one of those who had to be rushed to hospital.

"As I was walking up the stairs after getting off the train, I noticed that I was losing consciousness, and the next thing I remember is waking up in an ambulance," Tago told us. "If I'd left the train any later I might have died."

It turned out this wasn't the first time that Tago had been in this kind of situation: he told us that in 1989 he'd been staying in a hotel room overlooking Tiananmen Square when the student-lead protests were taking place. He was trapped in the hotel for almost two days, and several bullets smashed the windows of his room.

On March 11, 2011, the day of the 9.1 magnitude earthquake that struck the northeast of Japan, Tago was with his family in a town on the Fukushima coast. "Fortunately, when the tsunami hit our house the water less than 2 feet (0.5 meters) deep. Even so, it was a horrifying experience. Lifelong friends who lived nearer the sea didn't survive to tell the tale. I was lucky again." Tago showed us photos on his mobile phone of his house in Fukushima, flooded with black water, and also of the exterior, where on the horizon you could see cars floating alongside houses that hadn't withstood the impact.

Even so, having spoken of these three episodes of bad luck — or good luck depending on how you look at them — Tago didn't allow himself to get overcome with sadness; he soon changed the subject and the dinner ended in laughter. On leaving the restaurant we went to sing and celebrate being alive at a karaoke club overlooking Tokyo Bay.

Tago's story reminded me of that of Tsutomo Yamaguchi, a Japanese engineer who was working for Mitsubishi during World War II and survived both the Hiroshima and Nagasaki atomic bombs. The day after the first bomb hit Hiroshima, he traveled, wounded, to Nagasaki and told his boss what had happened, but nobody believed him. Two days later the same thing happened in Nagasaki, and once again Tsutomu Yamaguchi survived to tell the tale.

In both cases he was two miles (three kilometers) from the epicenter of the blast; the bombs didn't kill him but left him with burns and other permanent injuries. He died in 2010 at the age of ninety-three.

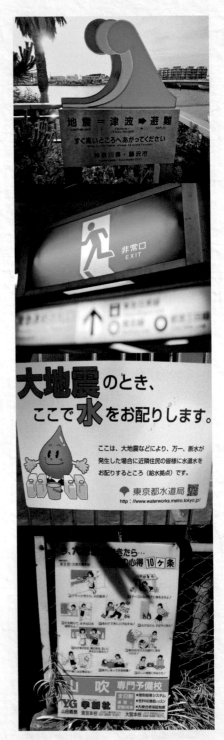

Warning and danger signs, including ones that give advice on what to do in case of disaster, are a constant feature of the Japanese urban landscape.

Characteristics of the Prism of Natural Disasters

- A conservative society, resistant to change
- When changes are made, these tend to follow the principle of *kaizen* (continuous and steady improvement) rather than rapid change
- Extreme planning
- Decisions are arrived at slowly
- All possible risks are calculated before any action is taken

This photograph of a ship that appears to have fallen from the sky was taken during my visit to the area of northern Japan devastated by the 2011 tsunami.

that could occur during the next few decades.

When a Japanese company or the Japanese government initiates a project, they usually prepare plans for ten, twenty or even a hundred years or more into the future. The level of detail is extraordinary. For the new maglev train that will connect Tokyo with Osaka at 300 miles (500 km) per hour, the plans show how profits will be generated from now to more than a hundred years hence, showing that it is good plan from an economic point of view for future generations.

The Japanese mindset considers all the possible ways in which entering into relations with an external organization could go wrong. From the negotiating perspective of the Japanese side, immediate economic benefits are a secondary consideration; the most important thing is to be sure, analyzing each risk factor obsessively so that it doesn't become a catastrophic problem in the future.

Where does it come from, this fixation with

analyzing every scenario in which things could go wrong — something that seems absurd or exaggerated to many outsiders? Those of us who live in Japan understand what it means to live in a land that is prone to being hit by major earthquakes. I'm almost certain that something primitive and biological is activated in populations that are under continual threat of annihilation by nature, making them inclined to analyze all possible risks in whatever context (not just natural disasters).

Fear lives inside the citizens. Though we may not suffer earthquakes every day, the subconscious mind of the inhabitants of this place is always prepared for the worst. This state of anxiety is transferred to other aspects of life and is what makes the Japanese cautious about everything.

In a negotiation, at the first sign of trouble, the Japanese side will refuse to sign, through fear and a deeply entrenched risk-averse mentality.

This behavior, which is so conservative, and always so focused on what can go badly instead of what can go well, was something that frustrated me, something I could never understand. I would ask myself: why aren't they more optimistic? Why don't they see the good rather than the bad?

But everything changed when I lived through the earthquake, tsunami and nuclear meltdown of 2011. I could feel the fear inside my skin. It was then that something deep inside me began to change, and now I'm much more risk averse than before in all facets of my life. Perhaps in this sense I've become a little Japanese.

Effects I've Noticed in Myself
- I've become much more of a planner than I was before. I believe that planning, more or less flexibly, is a way of mitigating the risks of things going wrong.
- I don't just consider the positive, I also bear in mind the negative in any new initiative I want to add to my life. Even so, I try not to be obsessive about the negative, I merely write it down to have it there. It's a kind of negative visualization, as championed by the Stoics in ancient Greece.

- I'm horrified at the lack of planning of certain American and European companies.
- I'm always checking where the emergency exits are in buildings.
- I have a survival kit at home, equipped with everything recommended by Shibuya Ward Office (including dried food and portable toilets) and the Tokyo Metropolitan Government Office, which would allow my wife and me to survive for more than a week in the event of a catastrophe or zombie attack.

Fear of any kind of risk extends beyond the world of business into all areas of Japanese society. For example, danger signs are more prevalent than in other countries, and evacuation routes and meeting points in case of earthquake and tsunami are always displayed very clearly.

On traveling to Japan, when you see signs which might seem absurd or exaggerated, don't be dismissive, try to analyze them through the Prism of Natural Disasters.

This obsession with planning also extends to the personal. For example, a group of Japanese friends are in the habit of holding a *hanami* cherry-blossom viewing party which consists of having a picnic and drinking sake under the flowering *sakura* trees we talked about in chapter 1. Their hanami is always in the same part of Yoyogi park. A couple of them always take the lead role in planning the hanami, using computer spreadsheets in which they include a map of each tree, seating arrangements for each of the guests, the exact location where each dish will be served, who is responsible for providing each item of food and drink, along with a detailed timetable. The picnic plan is more elaborate than some wedding plans I've seen.

When we use my system of Four Prisms to help us understand Japan better, we can at times fall into a certain reductionism. It's always a good idea to think things over and look at them from different perspectives. The obsession with planning in the extreme is perhaps not just a consequence of the fear of things going badly in the future due to a

MY PERSONAL ADVICE
How to Negotiate with the Japanese

An area of great frustration for foreigners is how to negotiate with the Japanese.

Why do the Japanese take so long to decide anything or to reply to something that seems so simple? Why don't they say clearly what they want? These are common complaints from Westerners.

Sometimes you get the feeling that they've rejected you, but what's usually happening is that they're contemplating how to respond. They're also thinking about the best way to answer you without hurting your feelings.

"I've been dealing with them for months and they seem interested but they won't give me a definite answer . . ." is a complaint I often hear. I usually explain that the best thing to do is to expect the answer "no," in order to avoid stress. The great thing is that if the Japanese side gives you the answer "yes," it will be a definite yes and you can rely on them completely. You can be certain that they will be excellent clients or partners.

These are my key tips for negotiating with the Japanese:

Reputation is very important. The Japanese won't risk anything that could damage their reputation. The economic benefit of working with you may not compensate for the possible risk of some scandal erupting in your company, for example. When you're making a presentation in a business meeting, be very clear that your

company has a good reputation.

When you present a plan, explain in detail how you are going to mitigate against all possible risks. Let them see that you are prepared for the worst. Plan even those things you think don't need to be planned, even if it seems like a waste of time. Do it just so they can believe in you.

Give them the maximum amount of information possible. For example, give them photos of your offices and tell them how the company was founded. Tell them who the managers are, what your long term objectives are . . . Give them as much information as you can. One thing I've noticed is that when the Japanese have a lot of information they feel *anshin* (calm) and are more open to carrying on with negotiations.

A new company employee learns how to negotiate by taking part in a roleplay exercise.

natural disaster. Another cause could be a heavy dependence on trains, with their detailed time-tables and their extreme punctuality. For example, in rural areas, away from the big Japanese cities, people tend to be more relaxed; they don't plan in as much detail as the people of Tokyo or Osaka, and they even arrive late for appointments. Sometimes you can guess whether a Japanese person has lived all their life in the city or not by their punctuality.

Another effect of the constant threat of natural disasters is that people live in the moment. This can be positive, but may also turn into something negative, because when taken to extremes it can lead to self-destructive habits. For instance, you see a lot of alcoholism in Tokyo. "What does it matter when tomorrow we might get hit by an earthquake?" is something I've heard from drunks.

Many aspects of Japan's feudal history are still present in the Japanese subconscious today.

The typical salaryman works during the day planning his work in the most minute detail as if he were going to live for ever, and at night he goes out to get drunk as if he wants to die. Both behaviors appear contradictory but I suspect that both are guided by a fear that everything is going to hell.

Some may ask why so much effort is taken to do things well if perhaps everything is going to be destroyed. But I would say that the average Japanese person (not everyone) makes a huge effort during the day to work hard and get ahead, but when they fall prey to tiredness and stress they end up seeing the other, more negative, side of the coin.

Why is Japan almost always governed by conservative political parties? You can now analyze and answer this question yourself using the Prism of Natural Disasters.

The Japanese are extremely risk averse and always have a certain fear of change. We can consider Japan to be a conservative society by default. People are very cautious when it comes to introducing change; in fact, they do so in such a methodical way that the form has become internationally known through the word *kaizen* (which is explained in detail in chapter 5 of my book *A Geek in Japan)*.

At first sight this seems to be a country that innovates at great speed, but if you look more carefully you realize that in many ways the improvements are always slow and cautious. This means that the Japanese often lose battles in the short term, but they generally win in the long run.

Although it takes the Japanese time to decide, plan and achieve change — because they're calculating all the possible risks through fear of things going wrong — when they do eventually pass from the planning phase to the execution phase they are unsurpassable and they don't look back.

The Prism of Feudal Structures

"Can you take the Caesar dressing off the salad on the menu and change it for olive oil?"

"Mmm," says the waiter.

He looks away, a serious expression on his face, and angles his head to one side. He utters another, even longer "Mmmmm . . ." and finally replies:

"Let me check and see if it's possible."

He walks away, almost running, toward the kitchen area and I can see him speaking to a waitress. After they've finished talking he comes back briskly to our table and says:

"It'll take a little while to confirm if we can change it. Let's carry on with the rest of the order for now."

When he's taken the order he goes back to the kitchen. A few minutes later I see him next to a man who seems at least twenty or thirty years older than him. They are talking at the kitchen door.

When they finish, the older man comes over to our table and after a deep bow, he says:

"We're very sorry, sir, but it's not possible to change the Caesar dressing for olive oil. But we can change it for this other dressing."

He shows me the last page of the menu where in small type it explains that it's possible to choose a lemon dressing.

"Thanks, but if there's no olive oil I'd rather have the salad without dressing," I reply with the best smile I can muster, noting the tension in his face. He's embarrassed that's he hasn't been able to meet the customer's wishes.

"We'll bring it without dressing, then. I'm very sorry," he says, with another couple of bows before returning to the kitchen area as quickly as he can.

He speaks again with the waiter who took our order and also with the waitress, no doubt to explain to them what's happening with my salad.

This is a frustrating situation, and one which, if truth be told, I have never got used to, but I amuse myself by analyzing it through the Prism of Feudal Structures. It's useful when it comes to putting into context any decision-making process, whether that's something as simple as changing a salad

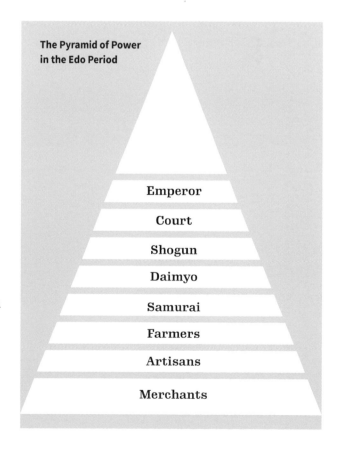

The Pyramid of Power in the Edo Period

Emperor

Court

Shogun

Daimyo

Samurai

Farmers

Artisans

Merchants

MAGICAL MOMENTS
Matsumoto Castle

We are traveling by the Azusa Limited Express train to the city of Matsumoto, in Nagano Prefecture. While crossing the Japan Alps and the green plains of Nagano, I am engrossed in *Taiko*, the historical novel by Eiji Yoshikawa, set at the end of the sixteenth century, when Matsumoto Castle was built.

The protagonist of the novel is daimyo Hideyoshi Toyotomi, considered to be one of the three unifiers of Japan along with Tokugawa Ieyasu and Oda Nobunaga. Early in the book, the following lines show the personalities of these three key figures in the history of Japan:

What happens if the bird doesn't sing?

"Kill it!" replies Oda Nobunaga.

"Make it want to sing," replies Hideyoshi Toyotomi.

"Wait," replies Tokugawa Ieyasu.

The novel includes the story of the siege of Inabayama Castle in which a young Hideyoshi Toyotomi, following the orders of Oda Nobunaga, plays a crucial role in defeating the Saito clan, becoming a kind

of hero in the process.

Though Matsumoto Castle doesn't appear in the novel, it ended up belonging to the territories controlled by Hideyoshi Toyotomi and Oda Nobunaga during the Azuchi-Momoyama period (1573–1600). In the year 1590, after defeating the Takeda clan, Hideyoshi

Toyotomi sent retainer Kazumasa Ishikawa to govern Matsumoto from the castle.

Matsumoto Castle has the nickname Crow Castle (烏城 *karasujo*) due to the black color of its walls and also because of the silhouette of its roofs that resemble the wings of a bird. From a

dressing or the signing of a multimillion dollar contract between large companies.

During the Edo period (1603–1868), all Japanese people were classified according to a pyramid structure of power (see diagram on page 37), the apex of which was dominated by the Emperor, the court and the shogun.

In this power structure, information always flows from subject to superior. In this way, the taking of important decisions moves up the pyramid of power as if it were a bubble floating to the surface. Once it gets to someone with sufficient power to decide, the orders cascade again to be carried out by those at lower levels.

Breaking this flow had terrible consequences — including death — and was considered treasonous.

Forming hierarchies of power is something engraved into our nature as human beings; the problem with Japan is that even today these structures continue to be as rigid as they were in antiquity. For example, in the work context, it is very much frowned upon to speak to someone in another department without your boss's permission. You must always follow the protocol of informing your superiors first.

In fact I myself, unintentionally, broke this traditional chain of command in one of the companies I worked for here in Tokyo, and the consequences were catastrophic. I informed my boss's boss about a small detail related to something I thought needed correcting in our company. The offense was such that they fired me from the distance, as you walk through the streets of the city, you can begin to make out the silhouette of the crow.

When you arrive in front of the castle it looks smaller than it did from a distance. It seems like a kind of wooden model that fell gently from the sky to end up reflected in the water which surrounds it.

If Mr. Casca was visiting the castle, he'd say things like: "What a useless castle!" or "They defended Matsumoto with this?" or "A single tower from a European castle is bigger than this." Whereas if Ms. Wonder was visiting she'd say: "How wonderful! It's minimalist and simple, as befits its function, perfect for watching over the whole region, and it's silhouette is unique and memorable. It's small but at the same time powerful."

Getting there Take the JR Azusa or Super Azusa train to Matsumoto from Tokyo's Shinjuku Station. There are one or two trains an hour and the journey takes about two and a half hours. The castle can be visited as a day trip from Tokyo, leaving early and returning in the evening, but it's better to spend a night in Matsumoto.

When you cross the red bridge and go inside, you realize that its interior is bigger than you imagine from outside. After I've finished exploring the inside, I find myself hypnotized by the sunset and the reflection of the castle's silhouette in the water, reminding me of the Golden Pavilion in Kyoto (see page 8). A pair of swans swim past, oblivious to my gaze, breaking the reflection of the "crow" for a few moments.

Control of the castle passed down through generations of Tokugawa daimyo for more than 280 years, until the feudal system was abolished in 1868. Today, Matsumoto Castle is considered one of Japan's most important castles and was named a National Treasure by the Japanese government in 1936.

LEFT Matsumoto Castle was named a National Treasure by the Japanese government in 1936. ABOVE Hideyoshi Toyotomi at the summit of Mount Inaba in the moonlight, carefully planning his attack on Matsumoto Castle.

company. I'll give a detailed account of the event in chapter 7, "The Dark Side of Japan."

The power structures of the Edo era remain a force to be reckoned with. The feudal world of daimyo and samurai no longer exists, but modern companies, the *kabushikigaisha* 株式会社, have types of structure and operation very similar to those that might have existed in a samurai castle three hundred years ago.

In companies, the flow of information is always from subject to superior, or from superior to subject. Communicating something by breaking the chain of command is considered to be very serious. It's difficult to explain just how strict the rules are in this regard, so I'm going to give you a real-life example from my own experience.

One day, after I'd just arrived in the office, the boss of another department sent me an email asking my permission to set up a meeting with me and one of the members of my department to deal with a "delicate matter." He was acting in accordance with the protocol of a hierarchical power structure.

The boss of the other department could have spoken directly with the member of my department as would have happened in any foreign company, but he didn't do so in order not to show disrespect in the traditional Japanese sense. I replied giving him permission to hold the meeting with us on the "delicate matter" and he responded, thanking me for my help in solving this "serious problem."

The next day, at the meeting, the boss of the

The entrance to the residence of a former feudal lord. The walls mark a separation from the rest of society.

other department informed me and one of our engineers that the big problem was that this engineer whistled from the moment he left the elevator until he arrived at his work station. The whistling was so loud that it was disturbing people working in the other department.

The mystery of the "delicate matter" was revealed, and the man guilty of the "crime" had to stop whistling on arriving at the office.

I can imagine a similar situation in any other part of the world being solved by saying to the person whistling: "Hey, buddy! Do you mind not whistling when you pass by our desks?" And then a few laughs and everything is settled.

Let's analyze what happened:

1. Engineers from department A complain to their boss about the whistling because it's disrespectful to approach the engineer from department B directly.
2. The boss of department A sends an email to me (the boss of department B).
3. I inform our engineer that there's a complaint from department B.
4. We hold a meeting where the engineer is informed of his crime in front of us.
5. The engineer stops whistling.

I have simplified this process. In reality, there are more managers and team leaders in the chain of command between the engineer and the departmental boss, creating even more obstacles.

When I asked to have my Caesar dressing replaced with olive oil in the restaurant, and when the employee was asked not to whistle at work, the protocols that were followed were hierarchical and quasi-medieval.

Despite having been here a long time, this rigidity of communication is something I've never accepted. I suspect that in this regard I'll always be a Mr. Casca. When the problem in front of you is solved, as for example with the whistling, it's not always such a big deal and you often end up laughing at the absurdity of the bureaucracy needed to resolve such a trivial problem.

But if you follow all the protocols and still don't arrive at a solution to a problem, this can be a source of great frustration. Although hierarchies may be necessary to organize a society, I believe

Characteristics of the Prism of Feudal Structures

- Dilution of responsibilities. Because there are so many steps on the pyramid of power, sometimes when something bad happens it's difficult to find one single responsible person.

- You always have to check with your superiors before making any change or exception that is not covered in the usual protocols.

- Gerontocratic society.

- Few opportunities for young people.

- Difficult to introduce change "from below." The rules governing how things are done are established from positions of power and people in other positions have virtually no authority to make changes. If the boss of the café has decided that they only serve green tea with milk, the wait staff cannot serve it without milk.

firmly that in order to live together harmoniously, it is fundamental that communication between all the members of a group of human beings should be open and without secrets.

It's refreshing to meet younger Japanese people born from the 1980s onward (a generation known as *yutori sedai*, "the relaxed generation," or *satori sedai*, "the enlightened generation") who break with the traditions I've just described. It's clear I'm not the only one who regards these ancestral hierarchies as diseases in Japanese society because of the way they block communication and the possibility of making decisions freely.

A healthy system should be more flexible in general — not pyramidal — and should make it easier for the most capable to make the decisions, rather than the most powerful or the oldest. New generations of young people are particularly

In feudal times, interior decor would have looked like this, with painted screen doors, paper window blinds, and tatami mats.

critical of the intransigent gerontocracy (*rogai* 老害) that stifles opportunity for others and that has established itself as much in private companies as in government.

Let's look at another real-life situation that might affect you if you are traveling in Japan, and which can be explained by looking at it through the Prism of Feudal Structures.

"I'd like a matcha tea," my friend Alberto asked a waitress in a café in Kyoto. "We don't have matcha tea but we can bring you a matcha latte," she replied kindly. "So I can't have green tea on its own? Can you bring me the matcha but without adding the milk?" Alberto responded. "I'm very sorry, but we only have matcha latte," the waitress repeated, looking embarrassed.

"How's it possible not to be able to have a green tea in Kyoto!" he complained to me once the waitress had left with the order.

I had to explain to him how difficult it is to change things that have been imposed from above. If the owner of the café has decided that they only serve matcha latte, then this is something that the waiters and waitresses don't have the authority to change, however upset the customer might be, or however reasonable a request might seem.

The subject of matcha latte is something that foreigners visiting Japan have complained about to me dozens of times — it's the Mr. Casca attitude in its purest form, failing to ask yourself what the real underlying reasons are for a particular situation. But I've never heard a Japanese person complain to me that they couldn't get a green tea without milk in a café.

"If you want a matcha or green tea the best thing to do is to go a place which specializes in green tea; normal cafés typically serve matcha latte, that's the way things are in Japan! Don't try to change Japanese things, they are what they are," a Japanese friend tells me when I explain to her the dilemma that many foreigners have when they fancy some tea.

The Prism of the Islands of Few Resources

Just like natural disasters, another fixed characteristic of Japan is that its entire territory consists of mountainous islands, with relatively little inhabitable land and scarce resources. In all, there are 6,852 islands in Japan. Having few resources has shaped Japanese society for thousands of years, from obvious things such as a cuisine centered on fish, to a widespread obsession with attention to detail.

Ingenuity and the capacity to make the most of very little are Japanese stereotypes, but they are quite close to reality. For centuries, Japanese meticulousness has been molded by scarce resources. This methodical trait spread more widely during industrialization, making Japanese corporations some of the most reliable in the world during the twentieth century. In time Japan became one of the biggest importers on the planet,

and also one of the biggest exporters, after making new products by adding value to what they had imported.

One day I arrange to meet my friend Suzuki to take photos in Tokyo's Ueno district. When he arrives at the entrance to the temple where we are meeting, he takes a bag of rice and a bag of oranges out of his backpack.

"My grandfather sent me twenty kilos [forty-four pounds] of rice and a load of oranges," Suzuki says to me, laughing as he takes the bags out. "I'm giving it away to friends. This kilo of rice is for you."

"Twenty kilos, what a bright idea to send that in the mail," I say.

"My grandfather loves sending me food."

"Thank him from me," I say, putting the rice in my backpack with my camera. "But you could easily buy the same rice in the store down the street, couldn't you?"

"Yes, you're right. But you can't find these oranges in Tokyo; try them, they're from Shizuoka Prefecture."

It's not only Suzuki's grandfather who sends food by mail, millions of Japanese people do it systematically. One of my wife's aunts is fond of

As one of Japan's most readily available resources throughout its history, fish is a fundamental part of the Japanese diet.

sending us vegetables whenever she can, sometimes so many that all we can do is share them with friends, just like Suzuki does with the things his grandfather sends him. Last summer she sent us a giant turnip so large that we couldn't get it into the fridge whole. We ended up having to cut it into pieces. We were eating turnip for months. The fear of being left without food is lodged in the Japanese subconscious and thus these apparently anachronistic traditions continue, even though it's a waste of resources.

But this obsessive perfectionism can create problems. For example, a question I've been asked hundreds of times is why do the Japanese wrap each of the cookies in a box individually? Sometimes the boxes hold barely ten cookies, often even fewer.

This is one of those cases where attention to detail has led to excessive waste. According to the Japanese way of thinking, each individual cookie is something so precious that it needs to be treated with the maximum level of detail — without worrying about the waste of the paper and plastic materials that are used for the wrapping. It's a contradiction: each cookie receives meticulous attention (one of the characteristics common to the Islands of Few Resources), but the consequence is that paper and plastic resources are being squandered needlessly.

In fact this isn't the only questionable behavior for an island nation whose major resource is the sea. To this day the Japanese are still hunting whales, as well as destroying the natural coastline by reclaiming land from the sea wherever they can. On occasion these reclamation projects are impressive works of engineering: Kansai International Airport, which is an entire artificial island, is a good example. But in other cases, coastlines are disfigured with ugly tetrapods. If you're interested in exploring these problems more deeply, I strongly recommend the books of Alex Kerr, particularly *Lost Japan*.

I hope that my examination of the Four Prisms of Japan can maybe help you to answer questions or solve mysteries that you come across on your

For some reason I still don't understand — perhaps because it's easy to grow in a small space — the daikon radish is abundant in Japan, and as popular in the family kitchen as at restaurants.

travels through Japan.

Let me leave you with a final question. I'm not sure whether it can be answered by looking at the Four Prisms, but maybe it's something you might like to think about. The question is, why do people share dishes in an izakaya bar-restaurant rather than ordering individually? In an izakaya the typical thing to do is to order large amounts and ask for small plates for everyone to share. This is customary not just in an izakaya, but also in other types of restaurant where they serve dinner. The central concept consists of sharing the same plate of food with everyone else. By contrast, in the West, at dinnertime the most traditional thing is for each person to choose their own dish.

One of the things the Japanese like when they travel to Spain is going out to eat tapas. Is it because it's such an easy way to share food with your fellow diners? Or is it because of the variety of foods that are offered to nibble at and share, just like in an izakaya or sushi restaurant? Or could it be related to the Four Prisms, and if so, which one?

Characteristics of the Prism of the Islands of Few Resources

- Attention to detail
- Maximum exploitation of space
- Meticulous recycling
- Collective is more important than individual
- Dependence on nuclear energy which led to the Fukushima disaster (although Japan is now moving toward renewable energy)
- Unnecessary mailing of food
- Artificial coastline
- Whale hunting
- Excessive wrapping of products of all types

A rainy evening in one of the many narrow lanes that run through the traditional Asakusa district of Tokyo.

A Summary of the Four Prisms

1. SAKOKU

Sakoku 鎖国 (鎖 chain, to enclose with chains; 国 territory, country) means "closed country." Japan was in sakoku from 1633 to 1853, allowing nobody to enter its territory. There are anecdotal exceptions of commercial shipping and special diplomatic missions, but these were unusual.

2. NATURAL DISASTERS

Within the territory of Japan there are more than one hundred active volcanoes and every year there are over 1,500 earthquakes. As well as this danger coming from inside the planet, Japan is also battered from the skies by dozens of typhoons each year.

3. FEUDAL STRUCTURES

For centuries, Japanese society was ruled by strictly hierarchical pyramid structures in which power was concentrated in the hands of either the shogun or the emperor, depending on the era.

4. FEW RESOURCES

Japan consists of 6,852 islands and its land is mostly mountains covered in forest, which makes the terrain difficult to exploit.

Throughout the book, I will refer to these four prisms as follows: the Sakoku Prism, the Prism of Natural Disasters, the Prism of Feudal Structures and the Prism of the Islands of Few Resources.

In Kyoto's Arashiyama a woman paints while a traditional rowing boat sails by.

"A cup of tea is a cup of peace."

—Nanbo Sokei

CHAPTER 3
Japanese Idiosyncrasies

In whatever part of the world we live in, we follow particular patterns of behavior. We don't know where they come from, but since we are accustomed to them from birth they seem normal to us. One of the reasons why travel is so fascinating is because we become aware of the great variety of behaviors to which the human being is capable of adapting. Ways of behaving to which we are unaccustomed might strike us as absurd, but a good traveler will look a little more closely and realize that behind everything there is an explanation. The good traveler will also realize that there will always be those who look at us as if we were the oddballs, and think that what we do is absurd.

Nekojita and the Art of Slurping

One of the first things I noticed on arriving in Asia is that table manners are very different than in the West. While I was taught that noisily slurping spaghetti or soup is bad manners, here it's not frowned upon. In fact, it's the exact opposite: in ramen restaurants you are supposed to eat noisily because it's a mark of respect for the chefs.

When you first go to a ramen restaurant in Japan and hear the slurping echoing off the walls, you might find it disgusting. Or maybe it will make you laugh, which was my initial reaction, but in time you'll find yourself getting used to it, and then you'll start doing it too.

The explanation behind this apparently grotesque behavior is a simple one: eating noodles floating in a bowl of soup with chopsticks is not easy; the best thing to do is to suck them up vigorously so they don't fall back into the bowl. This is the obvious

Green tea is served in a traditional tea house in Niigata. For the Japanese, presentation and location are as important as the food or drink being served.

Chefs in ramen restaurants are usually next to the counter. You see them cook and they see you eat. If you eat noisily you're showing respect for their work, letting them know they you're enjoying what you eat.

My Top Five Ramen Places in Tokyo

I always advise anyone who asks me for restaurant recommendations to follow their instincts and go into any place which grabs their attention. The quantity of good restaurants in Japan is practically infinite and you're just as likely to find good food by chance as in a restaurant you've planned to eat at. Having said that, here's a list of some of the best ramen joints in Tokyo:

■ **RAMEN JIRO** is one of Tokyo's most traditional ramen spots, and has been in operation for decades. It's famous not just for the flavor and consistency of the *men* (noodles), but for the quantity of *moyashi* (bean sprouts) they put in the bowl. Business magnate Elon Musk had dinner here on a visit to Tokyo. Ramen Jiro has various outlets, but the easiest to find is the branch in Kabukicho in Shinjuku, just behind the Hotel Gracery, which is easily identified by the Godzilla poking its head from the top of the building.
2-37-5, Shinjuku-ku, Tokyo, 160-0021. Tel: 03-3205-1726

■ **AOBA RAMEN** is a Tokyo ramen restaurant well known for its traditional flavor, and is recommended by ramen connoisseurs. It's one of the first ramen restaurants I ate in when I arrived in Japan in 2004. I didn't go there intentionally, however, and I had no idea it was a famous place. I came across it while wandering around Tokyo's Nakano neighborhood and decided to go in because the smell coming down the street from the bubbling vats of soup was mouthwatering. Aoba Ramen has various branches in Tokyo, but the main one is the Aoba Nakano Honten.
5-58-1 Nakano, Nakano-ku, Tokyo, 164-0001. Telephone: 03-3388-5552

■ **NAKIRYU** is near Otsuka Station and is one of the few ramen restaurants that has a Michelin star.
2-34-10 Minamiotsuka, Toshima-ku, Tokyo, 170-0005. Tel: 03-6304-1811

■ **MENDOKORO HARU** is one of the most popular restaurants among ramen otaku (ramen aficionados) in Tokyo.
1-11-7, Shitaya, Taito-ku, Tokyo, 110-0004. Tel: 03-3847-8553

■ **TORIPAITAN KAGEYAMA** is famous for its lemon and chicken broth, which is one of the most talked about dishes in ramen magazines in recent years.
1-4-18 Takadanobaba, Shinjuku-ku, Tokyo, 169-0075. Tel: 03-6457-3160

Ramen places tend to be tiny. It's not good manners to linger after eating because you have to make way for the next customer. In the lower photo, notice the ticket machine, where you pay for your food before you enter: when you go in, you don't even have to order, just hand over your ticket.

MY TRAVEL TIPS
Ramen Etiquette

If you go into a ramen restaurant during peak periods, don't stay and talk at the table once your bowl is empty. You should free the table for the next customers. These restaurants serve cheap food and their survival depends on the number of customers they serve each day. You don't have to hurry your food, but don't sit and chat with your friends once you've finished.

THE WORD "RAMEN"

Ramen can be written in hiragana as らーめん, or in katakana as ラーメン. Can you find the word in any of the photos on the previous pages? The word ramen originated at the start of the twentieth century when the first "Chinese noodle" shop opened in Asakusa in Tokyo and the Chinese word 拉麺 (*lamian*, pulled noodles) was transcribed as ラーメン.

reason, easy to comprehend with our Western minds, but if you ask the Japanese they'll tell you that ramen tastes better if you eat it quickly while it's still hot. So that you don't burn your mouth and tongue, the best thing to do is to swallow it as quickly as you can.

This is something that many of us foreigners are incapable of adapting to because we are *nekojita* (猫舌, where the first character 猫 *neko* means "cat," and the second 舌 *jita* means "tongue"), which means you can't bear having very hot food in your mouth, however quickly you try to get it down. And

LEFT **Five workers supervise roadworks. In other countries there might be nothing more than a danger sign.**
RIGHT **An exit door of a skyscraper is staffed by a security guard and three further employees waiting to offer any help needed.**

it's not just foreigners – there are also Japanese people who suffer from "cat's tongue."

Absurd Jobs?

Another typical initial observation that travelers make when they first arrive in Japan is that there are large numbers of people doing seemingly unnecessary jobs. When I arrived, I took a collection of photos of this phenomenon of superfluous work, but in a very short time I realized that it was so commonplace that it was futile to document it. I could spend a whole day taking photos of workers staring into space. On the positive side, it struck me that this is perhaps one of the reasons why the unemployment rate in Japan is so low.

For example, a bar that would be staffed by one

or two bartenders in another country might have four, five or even more people behind the counter in Japan. This phenomenon is also noticeable in convenience stores, where there's almost always someone ready to serve you immediately.

In clothing stores sometimes you'll find one person whose job it is to put the items you've bought into a bag and another person whose job is to take your payment. In luxury clothes stores the usual thing is to see more sales staff than customers, and you wonder how the business earns enough money to pay the salaries of the employees.

But the most obvious example of this phenomenon can be seen when construction or roadworks are taking place in the street. There is an abundance of supervisors whose jobs consist of simply warning passersby or drivers about the building work. On occasion you see four or five people guarding a manhole where elsewhere a sign would suffice.

Why are there so many workers for jobs which could apparently be done with fewer staff? I don't have a simple answer to this question. Perhaps it's a consequence of extreme specialization of workers. In shops and bars maybe there are so many staff because of the obsession with good customer service. As for roadworks supervisors, perhaps it's a consequence of being as careful as possible in the face of risk (see the Prism of Natural Disasters in chapter 2).

Queues

Coming across queues of people lining up perfectly is a phenomenon which I would say is much more common in Japan than in other countries. Sometimes, even in deserted alleyways, you suddenly run into a queue which, if you follow it to the end, leads you to some famous restaurant or clothes store.

For example, in Harajuku there's a popcorn stall which for more than a decade has had an enormous queue every time I've passed by. Nearby, there's a "fruit sandwich" stall in front of which huge queues start to form from first thing in the morning.

Perhaps it's because waiting obediently in line doesn't bother the Japanese as much as it does the Spanish; by its very nature it seems absurd to us.

But I'm not at all sure of the reason why the Japanese form queues everywhere. Are the Spanish more rebellious and less inclined to follow orders? Does the education the Japanese receive make them more obedient? Do the Spanish have less patience? Do we feel that the reward doesn't justify the wait? Is it simply because Tokyo is so densely populated there is no choice but to queue? Or does being in a queue makes the Japanese feel part of a collective (see chapter 4)?

The truth is I don't have a good explanation; if

you have a theory that explains this behavior, send me an email.

Where the Streets Have No Name

This section is inspired by a talk given by my friend Derek Sivers (www.sive.rs/opposite).

Imagine you're walking around a city in your home country and a Japanese girl who's looking lost approaches you and asks: "I'm trying to get to [insert name of famous landmark], but I'm a bit lost. Could you tell me the number of this block?" Somewhat confused you give her the name of the street. To which the girl replies: "No, I don't want to know the name of this street, I want to know the number of this block." At that moment, you wonder what on earth is going on in the lost Japanese girl's head. For an instant you think about saying to her: "What world are you living in? What's all this about numbers and blocks?"

Now imagine a few months later you're walking around Tokyo and you've got lost trying to find a Shinto temple near Akihabara. You go up to a Japanese person and you ask them: "What's the name of this street?" The Japanese person looks at you, puzzled, and says: "The streets don't have names, but over there on the corner it tells you the number of the block." And as you feel the culture shock, you remember the poor Japanese girl who was wandering lost around your home city and you understand how she must have felt.

In Japan, streets are simply empty spaces between each block with no identity of their own. What can be identified are the blocks of buildings, via a system of three numbers: the first indicates the district: the second, the block; and the third, the building or house within the block. It's a way of structuring cities that's totally different from the rest of the world, but it's perfectly valid, it's just a question of getting to grips with it.

Which is easier to use, our typical Western system or the Japanese one? For humans, it depends which one you're used to, but for computers the Japanese way is better. Not having street names makes the addresses much shorter. For example, the address of a restaurant might be

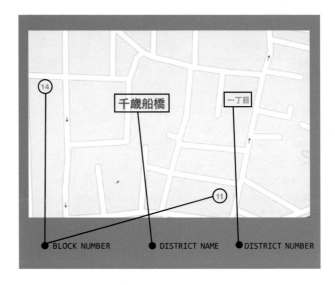

BLOCK NUMBER • DISTRICT NAME • DISTRICT NUMBER

"Sushi Sanmai, Tokyo, Yoyogi 4-3-1." As it's within Tokyo it could be shortened even further to "Yoyogi 4-3-1" and still contain the information necessary to find the exact location of the restaurant. Using these directions on a mobile phone or on the navigation system of a car is much easier than having to put in the whole street name.

In the address "Yoyogi 4-3-1," the word "Yoyogi" is the name of the neighborhood, the first number is the district, *chome* (丁目), the second number is the block, *ban* (舌), and the last number is the building within the block, *go* (号). The system varies somewhat according to city and region, but the basic concept of not using names is maintained. Only a few major thoroughfares or famous streets have names.

Where the Streets Have No Trash Cans

Last weekend I happened to be walking around the Aoyama neighborhood of Tokyo with Mr. Casca. After a good hike we went into a *konbini* convenience store to buy a couple of *onigiri* rice balls and a drink.

"Damn! I've got my hands full of trash again," said Mr. Casca after finishing the onigiri and his drink as we stood on a street corner. "What's wrong with this city — not a single trash can anywhere!"

"Don't be such a grouch. There's an explanation," I answered.

"It's such a pain having to carry your trash around every day."

"Everyone does it. Just look at how clean the streets are."

I then explained to Mr. Casca that the 1995 sarin gas terrorist attack on the Tokyo subway was carried out using gas canisters hidden in trash cans. Since then almost all the trash cans have disappeared from the streets of Japan.

When the Japanese are facing a big problem, one of the typical ways they have of approaching it is to try to cut it out at the root. Getting rid of trash cans is one example. Another, which isn't perhaps so noticeable, is that there are hardly any revolving doors since a fatal accident when a child was crushed to death a few years ago.

In reality there are in fact trash cans, but not in the obvious places they're usually found in other parts of the world. The general rule is that they can only be in private spaces – with the exception of the ones found next to vending machines, where bottles and cans can be thrown away– so don't expect to see them on the street. If it's your first time in Japan, these are the places where it's easiest to find them:

- In *konbini* convenience stores (always)
- Next to drink machines (only for bottles and cans)
- At motorway service areas (always)
- Inside private shopping malls (sometimes)
- In parks and gardens (sometimes)

Note: In Japan it's not the done thing to eat as you walk. The strange thing is that if you're standing still, you can eat what you want without being disrespectful.

TOP The sign tells people to take their trash home rather than throwing it away in the street.
MIDDLE and BOTTOM Look for the trash cans for bottles and cans in these two photos. Can you find them? They're usually next to drink machines

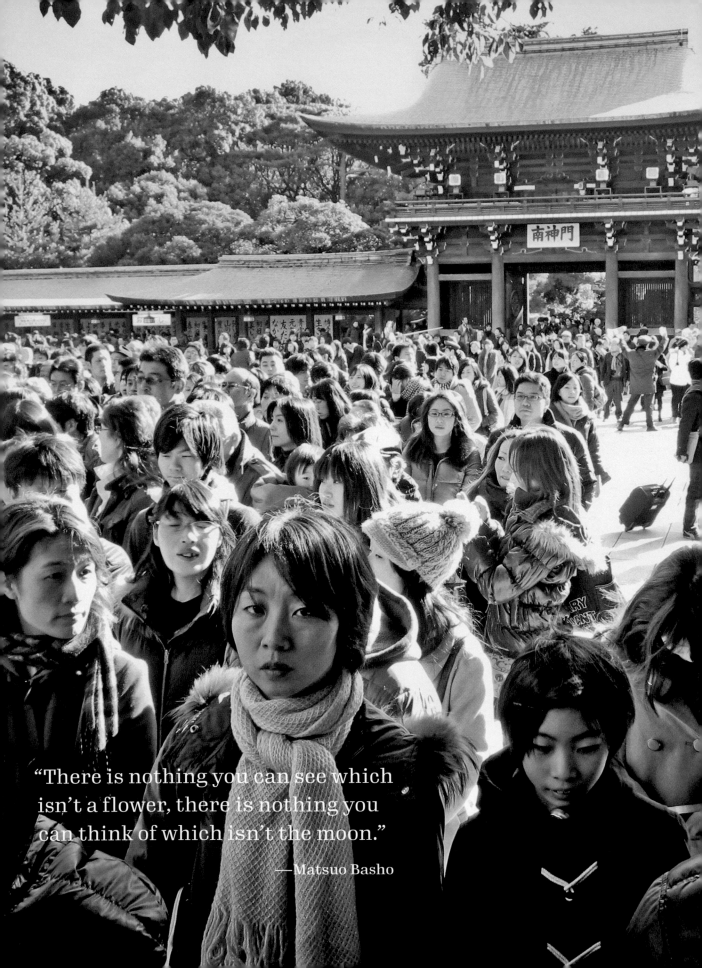

"There is nothing you can see which isn't a flower, there is nothing you can think of which isn't the moon."

—Matsuo Basho

CHAPTER 4
Key Cultural Concepts

In the first section of this chapter I'll introduce collectivism, an idea that explains the tendency of certain societies to collaborate to a greater degree among themselves and in general to act in groups. We can see Japanese collectivism through the Prism of the Islands of Few Resources described in chapter 2: having little at their disposal, the Japanese are used to working together, depending on each other, and working and living in a collective way.

Collectivism and Individualism

In Spain I never asked myself if I was living in a collectivist or an individualist society, nor was I interested in what this meant. Traveling and living in other places doesn't make you a better or worse person, but it helps you to gain other perspectives and to see things you didn't know about before.

One of the first things that caught my attention when I started living in Japan was the way the Japanese have of interacting with each other. In general they try not to stand out from each other and they tend to work as a group. This is something the Japanese are taught from a very young age. Two of the first proverbs you learn when you study Japanese are:

Nou aru taka wa tsume wo kakuso
能ある鷹は爪を隠す
Talented hawks hide their talons

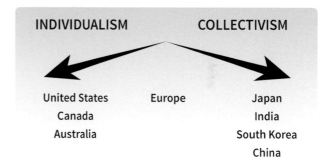

LEFT Crowds gather at Meiji Jingu shrine for *hatsumode*, the first shrine visit of the New Year. Note the order in the apparent chaos, with lines of people queueing up to pray. RIGHT A group of young festival goers pose for the camera using identical hand gestures.

Deru kui wa utareru
出る杭は打たれる
The stake that sticks up gets hammered down

LEFT This is typical behavior in a Tokyo nightclub,
with everyone facing the DJ.
RIGHT From a young age, the Japanese are educated not to
stand out. Wearing a similar uniform is a common feature of
both schools and the world of business.

I also noticed that despite a tendency to organize themselves into groups, the Japanese are still reserved when it comes to private matters. In Spain, and in Europe in general — especially in the south, we also like to mix in groups, but we're perhaps a little more individualist and we like to stand out from the rest. We like the feeling of being the best in the group, or we want our soccer team to be the champions. As far as privacy is concerned, Westerners tend to be more open-minded than the Japanese when it comes to mixing friends or acquaintances with family.

At the other end of the spectrum would be the United States, a society based on a more heightened individualism. Ayn Rand, the American novelist and philosopher, had this to say:

An individualist is a man who says: I will not run anyone's life — nor let anyone run mine. I will not rule nor be ruled. I will not be a master nor a slave. I will not sacrifice myself to anyone — nor sacrifice anyone to myself.

Perhaps it is more helpful to view individualism and collectivism as a continuous spectrum with particular characteristics, rather than as two things that are black and white.

Defining Individualism and Collectivism

In a collectivist society a great deal of emphasis and value is placed upon consulting with others when decisions are being made.

When I have worked in Japanese companies I have seen first-hand how misunderstandings can arise when negotiating with companies from other countries and cultures, such as the United States. For example, while the Japanese firm might be indecisive, spending weeks or even months on endless internal meetings to make certain that everyone is in agreement, the American company may have made a fresh start and be negotiating with other people, having forgotten all about the negotiations with the Japanese company.

This happened when I was working for a Japanese company with a subsidiary in New York, which was planning to open new offices in San Francisco. After several trips to the States and meetings here in Tokyo, several executives from the Japanese side were still thinking over the decision. The Japanese wanted to be sure that there was consensus among all the senior executives, sister companies and shareholders. To achieve this level of consensus takes time, and in the United States they were getting more and more impatient. After a few months, when in Japan we'd at last taken the final decision and went to communicate it to our subsidiary, it turns out they'd already gone ahead and signed a contract with another firm in San Francisco and were preparing to open the new office. The American side just didn't have the patience. The Japanese side tried so hard to get consensus that they arrived too late to make the offer to the Americans.

For Japanese people it's important to maintain harmony, *wa* (和) and to avoid direct confrontation, even if this slows things down when it comes to business deals. For Americans, time is money and decisions and risks are usually taken before consensus is reached with all sides, in an individualist way.

Generally speaking, in collectivist cultures there's more trust in other people than in individualist ones. For instance, studies of the behavior of online users show that in Japan and Korea people are more susceptible to being deceived when it comes to shopping online because they trust the web page or technology they're using, and tend not to think they're going to be cheated or betrayed. In the real world (i.e., not online) they're also too trusting, hence Japanese tourists are among the preferred targets of pickpockets abroad. By contrast, in the United States people are so individualist that it's the country with the greatest number of guns in the world; they don't even trust their neighbors.

A group of senior citizens take a group photo after visiting a flower garden.

Bureaucracy and Politics In Collectivism

Collectivism has its good points: Japanese businesses take longer to put all the moving parts in the right place in their search for consensus among everyone, but when they do manage to come to an agreement they are unstoppable — look at Toyota, Honda or Nissan. Though they may take time to make decisions, the ones they make usually propel them to the front line of worldwide innovation. They try to keep the company in a position of leadership at all times.

The problem comes when this mentality translates into avoiding any type of change, uncertainty or risk; it's here that we enter the world of bureaucracy and politics. Japanese bureaucracy is considered to be one of the slowest and most peculiar in the world. You could write entire books of anecdotes about Japanese bureaucracy and how simple decisions take years to take. The movie *Ikiru* (To live) by Akira Kurosawa is my recommendation if you want a more profound understanding of how bureaucracy works in this country.

I remember a story from Alex Kerr's book *Dogs and Demons*, in which he talked about a proposal to build a bridge to the mainland from a small island

At Tokyo's Shibuya Crossing it's fascinating to observe how large crowds of people can move without colliding with each other.

near Shikoku, inhabited by perhaps a hundred or so people. The project took so long to get off the ground that by the time the construction of the bridge started, the population of the island had shrunk by half, and by the time the bridge was complete, the island was deserted.

Japanese bureaucracy is slow, and once a decision is made things go ahead, regardless of whether it's a mistake or not.

I've also eventually realized that, although in theory there is freedom of the press in Japan, in reality it's controlled quite considerably by the state. Neighboring China could also be considered a collectivist society, with a government that tends to control the economic system and means of communication to transmit messages that can potentially instill a herd mentality. I wonder if this shared collectivist ideology is one of the reasons why these neighboring countries often fight over the smallest things.

In Spain we tend to contradict our leaders: it's a

healthy way to distance ourselves from collective thinking and to gain some perspective. We like to argue about politics and take opposing viewpoints.

In Japan – and I'd say in collectivist societies generally – people don't talk much about politics. I've talked about politics with Japanese people only on very rare occasions. People tend to follow their leaders through force of habit; if you say something which opposes the leadership you're automatically branded an odd character. On the other hand, if you start saying something out loud which more or less make sense you can quickly become a leader yourself.

Another of the negative effects of giving unconditional adulation to those who show leadership is a great proliferation of sects in Japan. This is a topic that Haruki Murakami writes about in his novel 1Q84, which I recommend reading.

Although it can be tempting to regard collectivism as bad, it can be a good thing when it's kept in balance and doesn't go to extremes.

Festival goers wear traditional clothes: *yukata* summer kimonos for females and *jinbei* top and trousers for males.

Group Dynamics in Japan

According to Dutch social psychologist Geert Hofstede, Japan is one of the world's most collectivist societies. Something I've noticed in general when it comes to group dynamics (although there are always exceptions) is that the Japanese tend to get together as much as they can but they don't hesitate to go their separate ways if a situation that could lead to conflict presents itself.

For example, when you go away on a work trip with a group of Japanese people, the team usually sticks together and decisions are taken together. But if at any given moment we find ourselves in a situation where, say, Ota wants to go to bed early to have enough energy to make the most of the following morning, and Yamamoto wants to go out to explore the area and go to a karaoke bar, the surest thing is that the group will separate without further discussion. Before any conflict or argument is created, separate plans are formulated: "OK, see you tomorrow at breakfast"; "Ota says he's going to bed, who fancies coming with me to a karaoke bar?"

Of course, if Yamamoto is more charismatic than Ota, he will get more members of the group to join him at the karaoke bar and Ota will go to bed on his own. Although the Japanese are capable of acting alone with barely any conflict, they tend to be weak in the face of peer pressure.

In a group of Spaniards I can imagine Pepe putting pressure on Alberto until he agrees to come to the karaoke bar even though he doesn't fancy it at all: "We've come all this way and you don't want to try karaoke?" "You're such a wimp"; "You're like an old man going to bed at eleven o'clock"; "You can sleep next week, right now we're all going to karaoke!"

I'm not saying that a group of Japanese people will split at the first sign of trouble, but it happens a lot. It's something that used to surprise me at

RIGHT Japanese people tend to copy
each other's gestures.
OPPOSITE Personal space is usually
respected as much as possible on trains.

first: we're going away
together and then we split up
for hours on end? This was
something unthinkable for
me, at least when I was in my
twenties; from our thirties
onward I suppose that we
Spanish are more grown up
when it comes to taking group
decisions, having become
more individualist, and we
don't have to be so close 100
percent of the time.

I'd say that we Spanish
tend to sacrifice ourselves for
the team, we want to be
together till the end, and we tend to form closed
circles. "Whoever goes home first is a loser."

When I try to explain to a Japanese person how
the Spanish are I usually say proudly: "If we are
family or close friends we stick together to the end
come what may."

I suppose it's not something black or white:
there are degrees of individualism or collectivism
which depend not only on culture, but also on the
environment we're brought up in. Were we raised in
a village or in a city? Do we come from a close
family? Do we live in an individualist or a collectivist culture?

**_Individualism or collectivism isn't a question of
black or white; the best way to consider the two
concepts is on a scale that takes into account not
just our culture, but also the environment we
live in and in which we're educated._**

Non-verbal Communication

It's said that 90 percent of the communication
between human beings is non-verbal. The way we
move, gesticulate, walk, respect the personal space
of others, our tone of voice and so on, are all key
signals we send to those around us, to communicate our state of mind and our role in the social
group we belong to.

After learning to get by in the Japanese language, the second challenge is to understand the
non-verbal communication of this place. Many
times, even when you've understood all the words
of a conversation, it's difficult to decode the
message or conclusion of what's been discussed
without understanding the context of the situation
and the non-verbal communication.

This is a problem not just for foreigners who live
in Japan, but also for the Japanese. Japanese
people use the expression _fun'iki ga yomenai hito_
(雰囲気が読めない人: literally, "a person who can't read
the atmosphere") to refer to people who don't
understand the social situation they're in and who
don't know how to read the context of what's
happening beyond the exchange of words.

For example, if a group of workers go out to eat
together after a week in which results have been
bad, the conversation during the meal might

revolve around ways to resolve or improve the processes used in the last project. If someone were to suddenly tell a rude joke or start talking about his or her family problems, this person would be considered some-one who is unable to "read the atmosphere."

In general, the *fun'iki* (atmosphere) has an emotional connection. If you go into a room and everyone is in silence, you have to be able to capture the emotion of introspection or sadness in the room, and stay silent yourself. If on the other hand the emotion sensed is one of joy and happiness, you have to adapt to the mood of celebration.

Of course, this happens to a degree in any culture. For example, in Spain there is often someone who is considered the joker in a group of friends, or there's an odd character who always seems to be out of place. What I like about the Spanish is that we enjoy having the joker or the oddball talking irrelevant nonsense even when the general state of mind doesn't warrant it. By con-trast in Japan, the person who is noticeably almost always out of place tends to be stigmatized.

We foreigners who live in Japan generally feel out of place, but we always have the excuse that we're foreigners and as such we have carte blanche to act outside of the consensus. It's not necessarily an unpleasant thing: sometimes it helps you to get your own way in situations where a Japanese person never would. When we use this cultural difference in a deliberate way, it's a technique that even has its own name: the *gaijin smash.*

Besides being collectivist, Japan is also consid-ered a high-context culture. In high-context cultures many things are left unsaid and are implicitly understood. In contrast, in order to communicate the same content, low-context cultures need to be more verbose.

You don't need to live in Japan to become aware of this fact. Reading works of literature or watch-ing Japanese movies we notice immediately that what is important is not what's been said, but what has been left unsaid, creating a feeling that stays with us, floating in our hearts.

There are two Japanese sayings which explain the importance of non-verbal communication:

Ichi ieba ju wakaru
一 いえば十わかる
Saying one is enough for ten to be understood

Ichi o kiite ju shiru
一 を聞いて十を知る
Hear one, know ten

In English the equivalent saying might be "half a word to a wise man is enough."

The Look

It is said that the eyes are the window to the soul. And the soul is something very personal. To gaze directly into someone's eyes can be considered an invasive act and a violation of privacy. It's as though you were poking around inside the other person's heart, or gossiping about their mobile phone messages.

The Japanese don't usually look people in the eye directly when they speak. Especially if they're talking to someone they're not close to, or to older people.

Silence

Japanese silence is a great mystery. At first it fascinated and worried me at the same time to see a group of twenty people sitting in a meeting room in silence. You meet up to talk about something and suddenly silence takes over the room and for a minute, or even several, everybody stares at the ceiling, looks through the window or closes their eyes as though they are deep in contemplation (or falling asleep).

Silence in situations in which you assume there ought to be conversation used to make me nervous. As the years have passed I've learned to accept silence. I still don't know what it means, but I no longer get anxious and I'm not waiting for someone to break it. On the contrary, silence gives me space to think and reflect.

Silence is perhaps a sign from the group as a whole that it's necessary to reflect on what is being talked about before carrying on. Normally silence presents itself when the group is facing a situation in which there's a difficult problem to solve.

In negotiations, silence is an element that has famously led to relations between American and Japanese companies breaking down. In the United States, silence is usually interpreted as lack of interest while over here it's not necessarily so.

Double Meanings

One of the first things the student of Japanese becomes aware of is the great quantity of polite interjections that are used to fill conversations. You switch on the television and sometimes you get the feeling that minutes have passed and the only thing that one of the participants in a debate has said is: *so, so desu ne, hai, so da yo ne, so so . . .* These are all expressions which lack meaning in themselves, but the way in which they are uttered can have an emotional effect on whatever is being communicated.

Take the word *hai*, for example. In the dictionary the official translation is "yes," but depending on tone and context it can simply mean "I'm listening to you, carry on speaking," or if the person you're talking to starts repeating *"hai, hai, hai"* in a less than lively way, maybe they're trying to say "I'm not interested in what you're saying" or "Be quiet."

Context, situation and intonation are everything.

OPPOSITE Non-verbal communication is key to understanding Japan LEFT It's important to respect each other's personal space.

Gestures

Japanese people are reluctant to show emotion in public. You're unlikely to come across couples kissing in the street, but that doesn't mean they don't love each other; in the context and privacy of their homes they behave completely differently.

If a Japanese person puts on a poker face while you're talking it doesn't necessarily mean they have no interest in what you're saying. They may well be interested but are reluctant to show emotion overtly. Their gestures are subtle, always restrained, and almost never explicit. While we in the south of Europe tend to move our arms and our bodies when we speak, in Japan you see less body language in conversations.

Knowing how to read expressionless faces isn't easy, but it's important. For example, it's difficult to get a definite no from a Japanese person, and sometimes it's frustrating if you're looking for a clear and quick affirmation or negation in order to go ahead with a decision.

Physical Contact and Personal Space

It's important to respect everybody's personal space. Not keeping your distance, for example touching the other person on the shoulder or drawing too close when speaking, can put the other person on the defensive. These behaviors might be viewed as a sign of connection and friendship in our home countries, but in Japan they can be seen as a threat or a lack of consideration.

The Japanese don't tend to show their feelings through physical contact in public places. Even when saying goodbye to someone close, there is no kissing in public. A typical farewell between Japanese people, for instance on a station platform, is simply to smile and bow instead of kissing or hugging as we would do in the West.

Context Is Everything

Nothing I've written about non-verbal communication applies in situations where alcohol takes control. Personal distance is not maintained, people look each other straight in the eye, silence disappears, all formality is left to one side, kisses are exchanged in dark alleyways . . .

For the Japanese, context is everything. If you manage to find an explanation for one kind of

お辞儀 The Japanese Bow

The bow, *ojigi* お辞儀, is one of the Japanese customs which most surprise you when you visit Japan for the first time. It's used in a wide range of situations from greeting people, saying goodbye, to expressing gratitude, apologizing, introducing yourself for the first time, to beginning and ending a ceremony or meeting.

For foreigners, it doesn't matter if you make a mistake when bowing, but knowing a couple of tricks will help you make a better impression on the Japanese people you meet during your stay in Japan.

If you're a man, bring your hands to the sides of your thighs and make a bow keeping your back as straight as possible. If you're a woman, bring the hands together just below the belly and make the bow, trying also not to bend the back.

The deeper the bow, the more polite and respectful it is. Bows are divided into three general categories:

会釈 *eshaku* fifteen degrees, looking at the floor ten feet (three meters) away.

敬礼 *keirei* thirty degrees, looking five feet (1.5 meters) away.

最敬礼 *saikeirei* forty-five degrees, looking three feet (one meter) away.

Bows deeper than forty-five degrees are not usually made. Beyond forty-five degrees we're entering into special categories where the bow is used to apologize for something, rather than a greeting or expression of respect. These sorts of exagger-

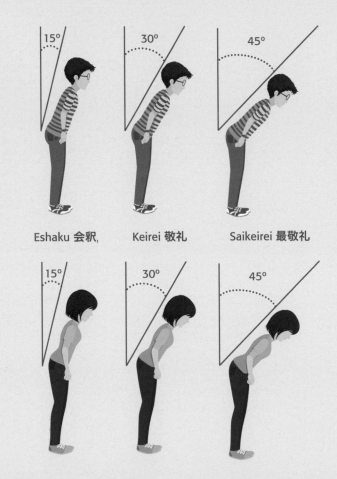

Eshaku 会釈, Keirei 敬礼 Saikeirei 最敬礼

ated bows are sometimes seen at work when a colleague has put his or her foot in it badly or on television when some political or corruption scandal emerges.

In extreme cases the *dogeza* 土下座 bow is used, when you have to kneel down and incline the whole body until the chest and the nose touch the floor, to express maximum repentance and remorse. It's also used in formal situations to show

respect, or in ceremonies such as Buddhist funerals.

There are many other types of bow, for example the ones used in martial arts, or the *zarei* 座礼, made in a seated position during the tea ceremony. But if you choose one of the three main types of bow described here, you will cover more than 90 percent of the situations you'll meet in Japan.

behavior in a particular context, it may well fall apart in another.

The Old and the New

The Bank of Korea carried out a study to better understand the common factors that make some of the world's oldest established companies so long lasting. According to the study there are 5,586 companies that have been around for more than 200 years, of which 3,146 are in Japan. In second place is Germany with 837, and in third place Holland and France, with 196 each. In my native Spain there are only four companies more than 200 years old, all of them distilleries: Raventós, Can Bonastre, Codorniu and Chivite.

It appears that one of the key factors for a company to stay in business for decades is the number of people who work there. It turns out that 90 percent of companies with more than 100 years of history have fewer than 300 employees.

Another common factor among long-lasting companies is that they all seem to be run by families for whom the most important thing is not simply to make money. What is important is that the business survives from generation to generation and is of some benefit to the community, employees and customers.

These factors are especially important to the Japanese, but some people criticize this as one of the problems that has held Japan back over recent years. A commonly heard view is "companies must die and be born for the country to progress." The opposing view, also often heard is "the stability and strength of our companies makes the Japanese economy resilient in the long term."

Right now, the longest-lasting companies in Japan are in construction, catering, metallurgy

A Japanese salaryman begins his homeward commute at Shibuya Station.

夏の思い出が、IUから始まった…。

アイユー

Passengers at Shibuya Station are pictured heading for the platform of the Yamanote Line (one of the busiest train lines in the world).

and the service sector. I wonder what the list will look like in two hundred years' time. And I wonder too whether the list of longest-lasting companies in the word will still be filled with Japanese firms centuries from now.

Hansei: Self-reflection

Hansei 反省 is one of the concepts of Japanese culture I've had the most difficulty understanding in depth, and I think I still have a way to go before I can really understand and coexist with it. But for the Japanese,it's a concept they are taught practically from the day they start their education.

Han 反 means "change," "to think something over" or "to see something in a different way," and *sei* 省 means "review" or "reflect on." The translation of *hansei* is usually "reflection" or "introspection."

All humans practice hansei to a greater or lesser degree, but let's look at the way it's applied in Japanese society.

The first time I was aware of the word was when our boss convened a *hansei-kai*, in other words, a meeting to "do hansei." I looked up the word *hansei* in the dictionary, but given its literal meaning of "introspection," I really couldn't work out what was going to happen in the meeting.

It started with long faces. The boss gave us a sermon about how serious the mistake we'd made two days earlier had been and that it couldn't happen again. When he said this I started to understand the "reflection" and "introspection" part of hansei. The thing is, my Spanish mentality – the Mr. Casca mentality – made me think: "But we all know that it was Yamamoto's error that brought down the production systems. The person who should be reflecting on what happened is Yamamoto and not us." I merely thought this, but said nothing, and I'm sure the others must have thought the same, but they also stayed silent.

Yamamoto was sitting at a corner of the table, eyes down, also in silence and listening to the boss's sermon. When he'd finished, the boss asked each of us why we thought we'd gone wrong and what measures we ought to take so that it didn't happen again. We all responded without mentioning Yamamoto, talking above all about the changes we could introduce into our team systems to improve quality control.

When it was his turn, Yamamoto apologized briefly with a simple *sumimasen* (I'm sorry), accepting responsibility. He then explained what he'd done wrong and what measures he would take to ensure it didn't happen again. At the end of the meeting, the boss wrote his notes on the board and said he'd send an email with the conclusions made at the meeting and a summary of the changes we should introduce in the way we worked as a group.

Later, the boss went to the chairman to explain what had happened, accepting all responsibility himself for the mistake our team had made without mentioning Yamamoto once. Yamamoto never made that mistake again, nor did the rest of us: thanks to the hansei meeting, we improved as a team.

I learned something else about the concept of hansei. The aim wasn't for Yamamoto to apologize, nor was it to blame him: the main objective was for everyone to improve following the *kaizen* method of continuous improvement.

Generalizing somewhat, if a work team in the West had found themselves in a similar situation they would surely tend to blame Yamamoto, and then, depending on Yamamoto's character, he might blame someone else. Tensions would rise in the group relationship, then eventually people would forget what happened – until the same thing happened again.

In Western cultures, influenced by the Christian tradition, the concepts of guilt and sin are instilled in us from an early age. When we do something wrong or we make a mistake, we are tormented by feelings of guilt and sometimes we can't face up to what we have done.

By contrast, Japan is a society in which the greatest fear isn't guilt, but shame. Yamamoto felt ashamed because he had failed the group, we as a team felt shame for having failed the boss, and finally the boss felt shame because he had let everyone down.

We humans make mistakes, but our reaction to those mistakes depends not just on our personality, but on the culture in which we have been brought up. The first reaction of Japanese people is usually a deep sense of shame (*haji* 恥).

This initial feeling is managed by reflecting on what happened (hansei), by being fully aware of what has happened, and by sharing responsibility for the mistake with the group. This response can also be viewed as a consequence of the collectivist way of thinking that we examined in the first part of this chapter.

In other cultures we feel guilt before shame, and sometimes we try to hide our mistakes, so that the smallest number of people possible find out about them. A typical attitude is "Hide the shit, whether it's our shit or our group's shit, or even throw the shit at the guy next door."

At first, I just couldn't understand hansei. I though it was simply about taking responsibility and reflecting; thinking over what had happened and seeing it from several perspectives. But hansei really goes beyond reflection; it's closer to introspection and self-knowledge, the "self-awareness" of the Buddhist faith.

Let's look a little more closely at how hansei can bring about a deeper self-awareness. The process of hansei can be divided into three stages:

1. Reflection, introspection and taking responsibility.
2. Recognizing that there is a problem. Identifying the origin of the differences between what you wanted to achieve and what you actually achieved.
3. Committing yourself to making a series of changes to improve.

These steps can be applied as much to groups as they can to individuals. When Japanese boys and

samurai movies or manga like *Naruto* or *Dragon Ball*, where the master always demands more of his disciples, even when they've already excelled themselves?

I confess that at the beginning, when I was in full Spanish mode and was still quite the Mr. Casca, it annoyed me that nobody ever seemed completely happy even when everything was going exceptionally well. Now I think I've gotten used to it: my bosses are happy but they keep it to themselves, they say what they say because they want more from me and from my colleagues. Though we may have met our expectations or even exceeded them, we surely could have done even better. At workplace level I feel nobody is really ever satisfied; the Japanese act in pretty much the same way when things go well and when they go badly. We are in a continual state of improvement, which we can only maintain by being constantly on the alert for defects.

An American company celebrates a project that has exceeded expectations with champagne. A Japanese company celebrates too, but they'll also meet the next day to analyze how they could've done even better.

Toyota is one of the most rigorous companies when it comes to hansei. They're always having *hansei-kai* meetings, regardless of whether things are going well or badly. They're always reflecting on their processes and attempting to analyze what they can improve. One of the Toyota mottoes is "Not having problems is a problem."

In the West, we like to boast about the things we've done well. We expect to be rewarded for a job

girls are scolded for doing something wrong they are told *"hansei shinasai"* (Do hansei!). With only these words, the children know that they must take responsibility, recognize and explain the problem and that they need to change in the future in order not to make the same mistake again. It's not a question of punishing the child and making him or her feel guilty, it's a question of making it clear that nobody is perfect and that we can always improve as people if we put our minds to it.

Bit by bit I started to understand that hansei is always there, even when we haven't made a mistake. I feel that my boss is never completely satisfied, he always expects more from us as a team, he always expects more from me. Whenever he praises me, the next thing he does is criticize me in a constructive way.

He'll say something like: "Héctor, well done, thanks for all your hard work over the last few weeks. But, please try to think about how could you do things better next time." It's not that he's angry; what he wants is for us to improve, to be better people, to be a better team, a better company, a better Japan. Doesn't it remind you a little of those well done. In Japan, although there are also celebrations when things go well, almost always the emphasis is on not standing out, being humble and reflecting on ways to improve.

They say that experience is our best teacher; if we don't learn from it, our lives are spent in vain. The process of hansei helps to squeeze every last drop from the thing we call experience.

The ultimate aim of hansei is change for the better through a process of introspection, to learn more about ourselves, to learn to be better people and a better society.

In the wake of the 2011 earthquake, Japan is living through a process of hansei at national level, which includes government, construction companies, architects, nuclear power stations as well all citizens in general. The greatest hansei since the end of the war is being carried out.

At Toyota they're always improving their processes, whether things are going well or badly; for Toyota: "Not having problems is a problem."

Heijoshin: A Calm Mind

A long time ago, the legendary samurai Miyamoto Musashi was practicing zazen meditation on the banks of a river with his friend and Zen master Takuan Soho.

Suddenly, a deadly viper slithered out of the bushes in the direction of Takuan Soho. Miyamoto Musashi noticed, but didn't move or speak at all, because he knew that any movement might frighten the snake and make it attack his friend. The viper kept moving toward Takuan Soho and then started to move across his legs. Of course, Takuan noticed that the snake was sliding over his body, but reacted only by smiling.

The snake continued in the direction of Miya-

LEFT In Buddhism and martial arts, *heijoshin* is a term that could be translated as "presence of mind."
BELOW Note the order and balance of all the elements in the picture. The restaurant owners are also responsible for cleaning the street in front of their property.

The three characters above represent *heijoshin*, a state in which our hearts and minds are always balanced and peaceful.

moto Musashi. When it was close to him, it stopped and lifted its head ready to attack to samurai. But instead of attacking, it suddenly slithered quickly back into the bushes. Miyamoto Musashi didn't react at all.

"Are you alright?" said Takuan Soho.

"I've trained all my life so that no other human being should dare to attack me. I have reached my objective. All living things without exception fear me. Did you see how the snake fled when it sensed my presence?"

"Yes, I did," answered Takuan. "It didn't dare attack you and thanks to that, both you and the snake are still alive. And yet you seem sad. Why is that?"

"Because I am so strong that nobody wants to come near me. And for that reason I can never have real peace inside [*heijoshin*]," replied Musashi, watching the river flow. "Whereas you didn't fear the snake," he said in admiration. "And neither did the snake fear you. Your spirit is so calm, so

natural, that the snake treated you as if you were just another rock, as if you were a tree or the wind. People also accept you in this way."

Takuan Soho smiled and carried on meditating. Miyamoto Musashi went on to spend the rest of his days cultivating his spirit of heijoshin and writing books.

Heijoshin 平常心 (平 peace, stability; 常 always; 心 heart and mind) means "heart and mind in a normal state and always balanced and peaceful." In other words it describes a state of being that is "normal": a mind that is neither disturbed, nor worried, nor mulling things over endlessly. It could be translated as "presence of mind."

The term heijoshin is used a lot in martial arts, especially those in which a weapon is employed, for example iaido or kendo. In these martial arts the term *shikai* is also used, which can be translated as "the four things to avoid" in order to achieve a state of heijoshin. These four things are:

  kyo: surprise
  ku: fear
  gi: doubt
  waku: confusion

These emotions are all generated by our own thoughts and imagination. This is in our nature as human beings: we're afraid of confronting something new; from the fear arises doubt and out of doubt we begin to worry about how to manage a situation that has taken us by surprise and isn't what we expected. We end up in a downward spiral that leads us into a pit of confusion.

To be able to defeat our rival or to face up to a difficult situation, we first have to conquer our interior. By cultivating a state of heijoshin, we can face any situation with better self-control, not just in a martial arts encounter, but also in our daily lives.

There's a Japanese saying which goes: "Walk along the path of fear, go through the valley and the shadows of doubt, cross to the other side of the mountain of surprise, and bravely sail beyond the sea of confusion."

Heijoshin doesn't mean being without emotions, it's a state of habitual emotion, such as when you feel normally. We're not beings with superpowers, neither are we robots, we just need to be in an ordinary state.

— *Tohei Shihan, Aikido teacher*

Shoshin: A Childlike Heart

Shoshin is written 初心, where the character *sho* 初 means "start" or "beginning" and the character *shin* 初 means "heart" or "spirit." It's a Zen Buddhist concept that refers to the behavior and attitude of beginners, but it is also a useful lesson for people who consider themselves knowledgeable and experienced. Shoshin means trying to always keep the mentality of a beginner when it comes to observing the world, dealing with people or carrying out any kind of task.

Somebody with shoshin well integrated into their spirit is a person who isn't afraid to ask questions as though they were a child, even if they may know more about a particular subject than anyone else in the room.

I was once invited to spend the afternoon in the private house of one of the world's greatest masters of tea ceremony. For the first half hour of the conversation the master asked me questions about how I prepared green tea at home. Not knowing what to say to him I answered as best I could as his questions continued: how much of a tradition of tea drinking was there in Spain, what kinds of tea do Spanish people drink, etc.

After this initial conversation, he took the lead and showed me in great detail what the Japanese tea ceremony consisted of. But what I remember most about that afternoon is not the lesson he gave me, but his capacity for smiling and asking questions with the curiosity and excitement of a child. I sensed in him a sincere humility.

When we humans confront something new, be it something as simple as a new dish or an unknown place on our travels, or something more challenging such as a hobby or job we've just started, we usually have an open mind in order to get the

> ## How to Activate Your Inner Shoshin
>
> - Try explaining something you consider yourself expert in to someone who knows nothing about it.
> - Reread a book for beginners on a subject you consider yourself expert in
> - Practice something you know how to do but perhaps haven't done for a long time.
> - Interact with people that are outside your usual circle of friends.
> - Acquaint yourself with ideas that are outside your comfort zone, perhaps by reading a newspaper that has a different political persuasion from the one you usually read or one from a country you're not familiar with, or by following people with opposing ideas to yours on Twitter.
> - Think about first principles. Is there some law of physics which means that rockets can't land vertically?
> - If you feel that everyone in the room agrees with you, you're not in the right place to keep your mind young and inquisitive.

information we need. We ask questions, we listen and we learn, and each moment is filled with excitement.

But when we've been living in the same place for years, eating the same food, working in the same office, our minds become more closed and stubborn. We think we know everything, when in reality we still have much to learn. The anchors of our fixed beliefs become heavier and heavier but we enjoy the monotony of routine and comfort.

It's refreshing to come across people who do the opposite. People who've been in the same job for twenty or thirty years and are still questioning each detail as if it was their first day. People who go to a restaurant where they've been eating the same dish for years but are still excited about going and who savor every mouthful.

Zen Buddhist monk Shunryu Suzuki says that in the mind of the beginner there are many possibilities; in the mind of the expert, however, only a few remain. Who would you prefer to be, a beginner with a thousand roads to choose from or an expert, stubborn and set in his ways?

It's possible to be an expert in a particular field and yet maintain the mindset of the beginner, freeing yourself of the weight of arrogance. But it's one thing to talk about shoshin and another thing entirely to practice it.

One way of achieving shoshin is to maintain the mindset of a beginner, regardless of how long you've spent doing something. For example, a martial artist who's been training for thirty years still practices the same katas he or she learned on the first day of their career, no matter how much time has passed. He or she could decide not to practice them any more because they know them, but no, the disciplined martial artist rebels, using shoshin to combat this very human of tendencies, and carries on training with the beginner's mentality intact.

In the mind of the beginner there are many possibilities; in the expert's, only a few.

This way of thinking isn't limited to martial arts, it's something practical that we can all begin to apply to our daily lives, starting now. This is my two step method:

DETECT if you're acting on the basis of preconceptions. For example, you may notice that you're not listening to someone because you think you know more than they do, or you may hear yourself saying to yourself, "I already know this." Maybe you're doing things routinely, without enthusiasm and without paying attention to anything. Maybe you've noticed that the magic has disappeared from something you used to enjoy.

ACT in accordance with shoshin: the moment you detect the spirit of boredom or arrogance enveloping you as you engage in an activity, change from the comfort mindset to the shoshin mindset. What would a child do in this particular situation?

What questions would you need to ask if you were doing this for the first time?

When we act on the basis of shoshin, our minds are empty and open to receiving new information; they're not afraid of change; they're not calculating possible risks and problems at every moment.

The aim is to stop being slaves to the old habits and beliefs we have a tendency to accumulate.

After so many years in Tokyo I've become a little like the people who live here. I walk around Shibuya wrapped up in my thoughts without paying attention to the thousands of details that fascinate the first-time visitor.

To combat this state of lethargy, the tool I use to activate my inner shoshin is photography. It's a remedy that saves me from boredom; all I need to do is tap the camera icon on my smartphone as I'm walking down the street.

I find that as I search for my next photo, I tend to walk more slowly. Suddenly the aim isn't to get from point A to point B, it's about immortalizing the next scene. On occasion I've walked down the same street dozens of times, but I don't become aware of the presence of something until I awaken my sense of shoshin through photography, and find myself reacting to my surroundings with the kind of curiosity I had when I was a child.

The narrow and winding streets of Tokyo, and of Japanese cities in general, create a landscape that is constantly changing. There is always something visually interesting on every street corner, offering stimulation to the city stroller. This kind of experience is more difficult to come by in large modern cities in other parts of the world, such as the United States, where wide straight streets make everything monotonous and boring.

Walking around Tokyo and getting lost in its streets is an experience you can repeat over and over again. By keeping your shoshin state of mind, whether by using photography or merely walking slowly and observing, walking through the streets of Tokyo is something you'll never tire of.

These days, when I go back to Spain for a visit I'm surprised to find myself in a place that's much more magical than it was when I lived there; I see it all again through the eyes of a child. Perhaps this is thanks to Japan, perhaps it's because I've been away for so many years, perhaps it's thanks to photography, or perhaps it's because of my shoshin way of looking at things. I've realized that one of the reasons people like to travel to Japan so much is because it's a place where you're born again, you become a child again. Japan makes you curious about everything: you see posters in Japanese and you don't understand a thing; you see food in supermarkets and you're not sure what it is; you see people behaving in unfamiliar ways. Suddenly you're back to a time when your world was as yet unformed and everything seemed magical.

When you travel in Japan you're bombarded with questions that act like a revitalizing shoshin tonic. It's such an addictive feeling that people who've been to Japan develop a passion for this country that keeps them coming back over and over again.

In one way, writing this book is an exercise in activating my shoshin mindset, because it pushes me to appreciate and savor the magic of the country that is now my home.

When magicians perform tricks it's best never to discover how they're done, because that way they lose their appeal. This is what I feel Japan is, one great magic trick we'll never fully understand — and it's better that way.

Shoshin helps us to rekindle the childlike enthusiasm we tend to lose as we grow older.

"In the twilight rain, these flowers sparkle. It is a beautiful evening."

—Matsuo Basho

CHAPTER 5

The Japanese Spirit

The expressions yamato-damashii (大和魂, the great harmony or wa of the spirit) and yamato-gokoro (大和心, the great harmony of the heart) are used to refer to the common sense, national character, shared wisdom, and sensitivity of the Japanese people. Yamato-damashii expresses the quintessence of what it is to be Japanese, as well as the purity and strength of spirit to overcome any of life's challenges. There is evidence of the use of the expression yamato-damashii since the beginning of the eleventh century, when it appeared in The Tale of Genji, considered to be the first Japanese novel.

The Spirit of Yamato

In the eleventh century, the term *yamato-damashii* referred to the ability of the Japanese people to cope with everyday life. It was a kind of universal social conscience, based on ethical rules influenced by Chinese thinking, which was entering Japan through Buddhism and blending with the local Shinto religion. This universal conscience championed the preservation of harmony and the avoidance of conflict at all costs, embodied by the character 和 *wa*, which is found within the word 大和魂 (yamato-damashii).

Little by little, the meaning of yamoto-damashii evolved to become a sort of symbol of national identity. In the first half of the twentieth century the meaning of yamato-damashii was tainted by ultranationalists who used it as part of their propaganda campaigns.

Imperial lady-in-waiting Murasaki Shikibu, writing the eleventh-century novel *Tale of Genji*, where the expression *yamato-damashii* is used.

大和魂・大和心
Yamato-damashii and Yamato-gokoro

Understanding these two words is key to understanding the Japanese spirit. Both words start with the same characters and are distinguished by the final one.

Yamato-damashii (the great harmony of the spirit) is written 大和魂. The first character 大 means "great." The second character 和 means "peace," "harmony" or "absence of conflict"; when used alone it's pronounced *wa*. The third and final character 魂 means "spirit," "soul," or what in German is known as *geist*.

Yamato-gokoro (the great harmony of the heart) is written 大和心. The first and second characters are the same as in yamato-damashii. The final one, 心, means "heart."

The battleship Yamato (大和, written exactly like the yamato in yamato-damashii and meaning simply "great peace") belonged to the Imperial Japanese Navy, and was one of the most powerful warships ever built. It was an object of national pride, played a key role in the war in the Pacific, and was eventually destroyed by the Allied Forces. The irony is that instead of bringing great peace, it brought only death and destruction.

Yamato was also the name of the province where the emperor Jinmu (660–585 BC) founded Japan. It corresponds to present-day Nara Prefecture and part of Mie Prefecture.

The Yamato clan, originating from the province of the same name, were the first clan to control almost all of the island of Honshu in the fourth century AD. Their control extended to Ise Grand Shrine, one of the country's holiest sites, dedicated to Amaterasu, the sun goddess. Having control of the most important shrines and temples was a key political strategy at the time to control the flow of information from the authorities to the citizens.

大和・漢語・外来語
Yamato, Kango and Garaigo

The origins of almost all Japanese words can be divided into three main categories:

Yamato 大和 This describes words originating in Japan. For example *akai* (赤 red), *miru* (見 look), *hikari* (光 brightness), and *sakura* (桜 *cherry blossom*).

Kango 漢語 describes words originating in China. The first character 漢 signifies "Han dynasty" and the second character 語 means "word." Words in this category include *shoyu* 醤油 (soy sauce), *kyoshitsu* 教室 (classroom), *rashinban* 羅針盤 (compass), and *doro* 道路 (road).

Garaigo 外来語 (outside, come, words) describes words imported from other languages; these are the easiest to recognize for Westerners studying Japanese. For example: *miruku* ミルク (milk), and *teburu* テーブル (table).

The following is a series of techniques to help differentiate between kango and yamato words:

- Words which begin with *ra, ri, ru, re* and *ro* tend to be Chinese in origin, in other words, kango.

- Words with long vowels are usually also kango.

- Words which include a contracted *y* syllable, for example *kya, kyu, kyo, nya, nyu, nyo*, etc., also tend to be kango. Spoken Japanese from centuries ago didn't have these sounds.

MY TRAVEL TIPS
Sailing on the Himiko

Space Battleship Yamato is a science-fiction manga and anime by Leiji Matsumoto. The spaceship featured in Matsumoto's work recalls the battleship Yamato from the Second World War. Leiji Matsumoto also collaborated in the design of a passenger boat called Himiko which operates on the Sumida River and Tokyo Bay.

You can find information about timetables and available routes for the Himiko at suijobus.co.jp/en/

CURIOSITIES
The Yamato Black Cat

Yamato Transport is the largest transport company in Japan. The company is famous for its punctuality and for its black-cat logo. Things are going so well for Yamato that it has expanded operations to a number of overseas countries.

At that time, the Japanese considered Amaterasu, the sun goddess, to be a source of wisdom and authority. The image of Amaterasu was used across the outlying temples under the control of Ise Grand Shrine, thus strengthening the importance that citizens gave to the goddess.

The time came when Yamato was not just the name of a province and the clan that ruled it; its meaning expanded to refer to the territory we now know as Japan.

In antiquity, in the kingdoms of China, one of the words used to refer to Japan was 大倭 (*Oyamato*) in which 大 means "great" and 倭, which means "Japanese people."

It's interesting to note that in the beginning,

NADESHIKO JAPAN

This is the nickname of the women's national soccer team that won the World Cup in 2011. The name Nadeshiko is used symbolically to recall the phrase *yamato-nadeshiko*, which describes to the essence of Japanese womanhood.

the Chinese used 倭 in a derogatory way, with the meaning of "barbarian." But as time passed, the Japanese changed the second character for 和 (harmony), to become Yamato 大和.

Yamato-nadeshiko

Yamato-nadeshiko 大和撫子, where *nadeshiko* literally means "dianthus flowers" (more commonly known as pinks), is a term that is used to refer to the values and beauty of the ideal Japanese woman, or in general to the "perfect woman."

Its use currently is imbued with a strange nostalgia, since the characteristics of the supposed ideal woman, constructed according to somewhat macho traditional standards, have been disappearing over the last few generations.

The yamato-nadeshiko woman — in the traditional sense — is strong, faithful, humble, intelligent, feminine and kind; the family is the most important thing in her life and she's very skilful around the house. She must respect and obey her husband above all, and if she thinks he's made a mistake she has to try to find an indirect way of correcting it without him realizing, so as not to humiliate him. In the TV show *Yamato Nadeshiko*, the actress Nanako Matsushima acts out several situations in which she has to put right her future husband's behavior without him noticing.

During the Second World War, the term was also exploited in far-right propaganda. The woman with the "true" yamato-nadeshiko heart had to act for the benefit of the family and the nation. She had to give everything for her husband and to be prepared to die in the war if necessary, which would be considered an "honorable death" (玉砕 *gyokusai*).

The traditional, macho ideal of *yamato-nadeshiko* is becoming more and more outdated, and is being replaced by the ideal of a woman who is a both a heroine and a leader. From the answers I've received to questions I've asked of both women and men, the present-day ideal of yamato-nadeshiko womanhood is positive: a woman who's strong, courageous, acting on her own initiative, with clear ideas and leadership skills.

Japanese animator Hayao Miyazaki tries to offer an updated image of yamato-nadeshiko through the heroic female characters who appear in his movies *Spirited Away* and *The Castle of Cagliostro*, among others.

The present-day ideal of womanhood associated with yamato-nadeshiko is positive: a woman who's strong, courageous, acting on her own initiative, with clear ideas and leadership skills.

Yamato-e

Yamato-e 大和絵, where the third character means "drawing" and the first two characters read *yamato,* is a style of Japanese art popular from the eighth to the twelfth centuries, inspired by Tang Dynasty painting from China.

Yamato-e art tends to highlight the beauty of nature and to represent scenes from everyday life. Sometimes yamato-e works include text that gives extra information about the scene represented in the drawing.

The *yamato-e* style is one of the foundations on which *ukiyo-e* woodblock prints and subsequently manga were developed.

Fujin Raijin: A Key Work of Japanese Art

The work *Fujin-Raijin-zu* by Tawaraya Sotatsu, painted at the start of the seventeenth century is considered to be the most important work of art in Japanese history.

The painting represents the gods Fujin 風神 (風 wind; 神 god), the god of wind and Raijin 雷神 (雷 thunder; 神 god), the god of storms. Both of the gods hail from Japanese mythology and they play a crucial part in the Japanese creation myth.

Legend has it that these two gods were wicked at first, and enemies of Buddha. But they were eventually captured and ended up succumbing to the forces of goodness. For example, Fujin took charge of cleaning the cosmos, creating a huge gust of wind that helped the sunlight to reach the darkest corners of the universe. After this feat of cosmic cleaning, other gods, led by Amaterasu the sun goddess, began their own work to create the territory that would eventually come to be known as Japan.

Fujin and Raijin are friends; they are almost always together. Raijin likes to play the *taiko* drums to provoke storms, while Fujin enjoys adding a touch of typhoon wind to a storm by wafting an enormous sheet.

The artist of the famous painting of the two, Tawaraya Sotatsu, was one of the founders of the Rimpa school of Japanese painting. The work of this school is characterized by clearly outlined

A statue of Fujin, the god of wind, guarding the gates of a temple in Nikko.

figures on backgrounds of gold. The Rimpa school had a great influence on the art of the Edo period (1603–1868).

Two of Sotatsu's students, Ogata Korin and Hoitsu Sakai, copied his masterpiece. Thus there are three versions of *Fujin-Raijin-zu*. The three originals are almost identical but there are subtle differences in the versions by Sotatsu's students that make Fujin and Raijin seem more human than godlike. For example in the Sotatsu version the pupils of the gods' eyes are enormous, in the version by Ogata Korin they are medium-sized and in Hoitsu Sakai's, they're tiny.

Fans of video games who remember *Mortal Kombat* will be interested to know that the fighter Raiden is a slimmer version of the god of storms, Raijin. Fujin and Raijin also appear in the game *Final Fantasy VIII* and in the anime and manga *Naruto*, in which one of the "stupid brothers" is called Fujin.

The Soul Is in the Belly

Ancient philosophies and religions from India and China that influenced almost all of Asia, consider humans to be a union of spirit and body: the union of yin and yang, and of energy, ki, which gives life to the body. This energy flows from the body's center of gravity, which is in the belly (腹 *hara*).

For the Japanese the belly is the center of the body and the source of the life force, ki. In Western philosophies we speak of searching for the balance between reason and the feelings which flow from the heart; in the case of the East you have to look for the balance between reason and the ki energy which emerges near the belly button. In the West, when we speak about ourselves, sometimes we beat or place our hand on our chest, where the heart is. In Japan, they place their hands on their belly to indicate the self. This has been a tradition for thousands of years, but it seems to be disappearing and in recent times young people place a finger on the end of the nose. But you'll never see a Japanese person putting their hand on their heart to signify the self.

The samurai were influenced by Confucianism, Taoism and Shinto. For the samurai, as for all Japanese, the spirit — the center from which the *ki* circulates — is in the stomach. The traditional samurai suicide ritual of *seppuku* or *harakiri* consists of disemboweling oneself just below the stomach. The word *seppuku* 切腹 is written using the characters 切 (cut) and 腹 (belly, stomach). The word *harakiri* has the same meaning and uses the same characters (in reverse order) but is more colloquial.

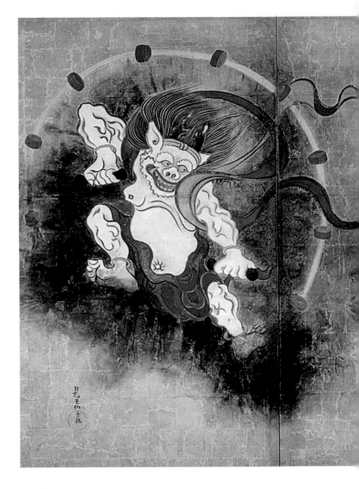

The painting *Fujin-Raijin-zu*, depicting the gods Fujin and Raijin, is one of the most important works in the history of Japanese art.

Fans of the anime and manga *Naruto* will have seen pictures of how the ki flows from the body's center of gravity in the belly. And for those of you who practice meditation, the navel chakra may vary in importance, but is always present.

In the Japanese language you can find lots of references to the belly as the center of gravity of the human body, and even as a part of the body capable of making its own decisions.

I remember when my friend Hiyama said to me: "My belly's up on its feet with what happened yesterday with a friend of mine." I couldn't work out if something good or bad had happened. Hiyama realized that I hadn't understood and explained to

me that *haradatsu* 腹立つ means "to get angry," but the literal translation of the characters would be "the stomach gets to its feet or stands up." He also explained another usage of the word: *hara wo kimeru* 腹を決める which means "to decide completely," but the literal translation would be "to decide the stomach."

I'm giving you a series of examples to show you just how flexible the use of the word belly is. Pay particular attention to the literal translations, which will give you an idea of the real sense of the expressions:

- *Hara wo sueru* 腹を据える: to decide. Literal translation: to decide with the stomach.
- *Haradokei* 腹時計: internal clock. Literal translation: the clock of the stomach.
- *Haradumari* 腹積もり: plan. Literal translation:

plan which has been decided on with the stomach more than with the head.

- *Haraise* 腹いせ: revenge. Literal translation : to cure the stomach.
- *Hara ga dekiteiru* 腹ができてる: to be ready for anything. Literal translation: to have a full belly.
- *Hara wo neru* 腹を練る: to turn something over in your mind, to think about something a lot. Literal translation: to knead or roll out the stomach.

For the Japanese, the soul or spirit is situated in the belly, around the belly button.

"The summer moon,
Paper lanterns on the street."

—Masaoka Shiki

Religion in Japan

Buddhism and Shinto are the two great religions of Japan. Shinto is as old as the tribal culture that eventually formed Yamato (the ancient name for Japan). Buddhism was imported from the Qi Empire and the Northern Wei Empire (present-day China) from the sixth century onward.

Both religions have coexisted in harmony for the most part. In some periods, however, nationalist initiatives were launched to reduce the influence of Buddhism, including from time to time the destruction of temples. Following the rebuilding of Japan since the end of the Second World War, official estimates show that there are a hundred thousand Shinto shrines and seventy-five thousand Buddhist temples in the country.

The wife of a friend of mine recently traveled around Japan. After visiting her first temple she asked me: "And do the Japanese believe, or not?" I answered, but without really giving a clear reply: "Here it's not a question of believing or not believing." My friend laughed at me, saying that I was turning Japanese.

Shinto and Buddhism

In Japan, religions, rituals, spirits, demons, and gods mingle together in a blend of tones and traditions; there is no clear division between "believing" and "not believing."

Despite the sheer quantity of shrines and temples and the coexistence of different religions, the majority of Japanese people don't identify with any religion. According to the results of a survey carried out in 2008 by the NHK Broadcasting Culture Research Institute, barely 39 percent of Japanese consider themselves religious.

Of that 39 percent, 51 percent said they identify as Shinto, 35 percent as Buddhist, and the rest with other religions. This leaves us with 61 percent of the population who identify with no religion.

LEFT A young man plays a *taiko* drum at a local festival.
BELOW A red *torii* gate marks the entrance to a shrine.

Photos taken after dark of the Kameido Tenjin shrine in the east of Tokyo. It's a ten minute walk north of Kameido Station on the Sobu train line.

Looking at data obtained from surveys like this one, you might get the impression that the Japanese are lacking in spirituality and unaware of their religious traditions. Nothing could be further from the truth, however.

Though 61 percent of people don't identify with any specific religion, the majority practice them at key moments in their lives.

If the surveys had asked — did you follow the Shinto *hatsumode* shrine-visiting tradition at the beginning of the year? Where and how did you get married? Which rituals did your family follow when you were born? Have you participated in a *matsuri* (festival) in the last year? Have you been to a Buddhist funeral? — I'd say that 99.99 percent of people would answer at least one of these questions in the affirmative. Although the Japanese may not identify with any particular religion, they do continually practice rituals from different religious traditions.

In fact, if I answer these questions, as an outsider living here and as someone who doesn't identify with any religion either, the results are

similar to those we'd get by asking a Japanese person — all except the first one:

Which rituals did your family follow when you were born? I was born in Spain. I had a Christian baptism.

Where and how did you get married? I got married in a shrine in the Shinto tradition. But at the reception we wore dinner jackets and my Japanese wife wore a Western wedding dress.

Have you been to a Buddhist funeral? Yes. At one of them I was one of the people chosen to follow the grisly ritual of picking the bones of the cremated dead person out of the ash using chopsticks. [This is why it's taboo to pass food from one person to another using chopsticks when you're eating.]

Did you follow the Shinto hatsumode shrine-visiting tradition at the beginning of the year? Yes. [Hatsumode is a tradition followed during the first few days of the year. You simply go to your favorite shrine and ask the gods for good luck for the year ahead]. It's the time of year when the shrines are at their busiest.

If you asked a Japanese person the same questions, the only difference would be the baptism — which is almost always Shinto — and perhaps also the wedding. Many Japanese people decide to omit the Shinto celebration and to get married in a Christian ceremony.

So, the pattern that the majority of Japanese people follow is:

- Shinto baptism (*miyamairi*)
- Shinto and/or Christian wedding (a widespread part-time job for foreigners in Japan is to officiate at Japanese Western-style weddings)
- Buddhist funeral

Another interesting fact, and one which surprised me when I heard it, is that 92 percent of CEOs of companies listed on the Japanese stock exchange have a *kamidana* (a kind of miniature Shinto shrine) in their office. We are again faced with a sort of contradiction, because the CEOs were also asked if they "believed" in Shinto and the majority answered no, but what they do believe is that having a kamidana in the office will improve sales for the company.

In the eyes of a Westerner who's not used to living in a society in which different traditions and religions are interwoven, this potpourri can be unsettling. It doesn't seem to bother the Japanese in the slightest. It isn't ideals or identifying with something specific that is important; the important thing is to celebrate events through the observation of rituals. The emphasis is placed more on traditional practice than on the beliefs themselves.

Shinto

Shinto 神道 (神 *kami,* spirits or gods; 道 road) is the indigenous religion of Japan. Its origins go back to the first settlers of the Japanese archipelago. Japan's first written historical records, the *Kojiki*

神 Spirits and Gods

Kami 神 is one of those words I'm reluctant to translate because no adequate word exists in our language with exactly the same meaning. (In Japanese there is no plural form, so kami is used to refer to one single spirit or to a multitude of them.)

The Japanese use kami to refer to:

- *spirits*
- *gods*
- *entities that inhabit nature*
- *the essence of something or someone*
- *the soul of something or someone*

According to the mythology of Shinto, kami don't live in another world or dimension, rather they cohabit with human beings and can manifest themselves in many ways; as rivers, animals, places, clothes, objects . . . one or several kami may even exist inside a computer or mobile phone.

For example, we can refer to the spiritual entity that is believed to inhabit Mount Fuji as a kami. We can also go to a Shinto shrine and pray to various kami for good luck in exams. Or, we can visit a shrine with technology kami where we can buy *omamori* amulets that have the power to help us avoid problems with our computers or mobile phones. One of these shrines is Kanda Myojin in Tokyo, a few minutes walk away from Ochanomizu Station and close to the Akihabara district of electronics retailers.

The variety of kami is practically endless. One of the most entertaining aspects of traveling through Japan is coming across shrines dedicated to every type of kami imaginable.

and the *Nihon Shoki*, dating from the eighth century, contain many of the ingredients, traditions and mythology upon which Shinto is based.

In Shinto, the emphasis is on the practice of ritual more than on beliefs or commandments. It makes little difference whether people believe in gods or spirits or not; what is important is that they carry out rituals as dictated by tradition.

Buddhism

Buddhism is built upon the principle that practitioners can achieve liberation from suffering. From the birth of Buddhism in India in the sixth century BC until its arrival in Japan, a thousand years passed. It arrived via Korea and China, where it had already been influenced and modified from its original form. At that time, very few Japanese people were able to read Buddhist scriptures, most of which were written in Chinese. Though only a few intellectuals understood the writings, the illiterate inhabitants of Japan were attracted to Buddhism through the statues of Buddha and Buddhist art in

LEFT *Torii* gateways are one of the distinctive ways of knowing that you're visiting a Shinto shrine.
RIGHT The *torii* entrance gate at Tokyo's Meiji Jingu shrine, one of the most important places of worship in the country.

general, which helped the religion to spread rapidly.

With the passage of time, Buddhism began to mutate, acquiring a style that was unique to Japan, and different sects were born. Currently the largest Buddhist sects or schools in Japan are Zen, Nichiren, Shingon and Amida.

The different sects and Buddhist institutions began to acquire such importance that the shogun started to use them as mechanisms for controlling and administering the country. For example, the first Japanese censuses were carried out using "temple certificates" (*terauke*) which every person had to obtain from their nearest Buddhist temple.

Buddhism is considered to be the second religion of Japan behind Shinto.

Gates and Entrances

The word *mon* 門 means door, entrance or gateway. When used in the context of sacred buildings it almost always refers to the gateway of a Buddhist temple. There are dozens of types of mon; the most important are the *sanmon* (*door of the three liberations*), which is made up of three sub-doors which, as you pass through them, represent liberation from greed, hate and ignorance.

寺・神社
Buddhist Temples and Shinto Shrines

In Japanese the word 寺 (*tera*) is used to refer to places of worship of Buddhist deities and the word 神社 (*jinja*) for Shinto ones. Buddhist temples and Shinto shrines are sometimes situated right next to each other, and can even merge into a kind of Buddhist-Shinto fusion.

In this book I use the following words:

- Shrine: to refer to Shinto places of worship
- Temple: to refer to Buddhist places of worship

BUDDHIST TEMPLES

- HAVE *MON* GATES, WHICH CAN BE OF VARIOUS SIZES, OFTEN WITH TWO STORIES AND CURVING TILED ROOFS

- MAY BE HIGHLY ORNATE, ESPECIALLY INSIDE

- SOMETIMES THERE IS A CEMETERY ATTACHED

- MAY HAVE PAGODAS OF SEVERAL STORIES

The pagodas of Buddhist temples can be very tall. The one pictured is at Asakusa temple in Tokyo.

Statues of Buddha, Kannon and other deities—usually in human form — are reliable indicators that you're visiting a Buddhist temple.

SHINTO SHRINES

- HAVE *TORII* GATES, WHICH ARE OFTEN WOODEN POSTS PAINTED RED. THEY CAN ALSO BE MADE OF STEEL, CONCRETE OR OTHER MATERIALS.

- SIMPLY DECORATED, BOTH INSIDE AND OUT

- GENERALLY HAVE NO CEMETERY

- USUALLY JUST ONE STORY

Shinto shrine buildings tend to be less ornate.

The *inari* fox is a typical Shinto *kami*, often found guarding the entrance to a Shinto shrine.

MAGICAL MOMENTS
Shinjuku's Hanazono Shrine

I'm walking past Yoyogi Station toward Shinjuku and suddenly the sky clouds over. People start opening their umbrellas as they come out of the station. Many of the umbrellas are the transparent ones you can see through as you walk.

Though today is the first day of spring, it has started to snow, a rare occurrence in Tokyo. I make the most of this unusual event by getting out my camera and heading for the *torii* gates of the Hanazono Shrine, hidden among the buildings of Shinjuku.

The snow falls more and more heavily. The white of the flakes contrasts with the orange tones of the torii. A pair of *koma-inu* lion-dog statues seem to stare at me while I take my photos.

As I get to the end of the passageway of torii gates that mark the entrance to the sacred part of the temple, I find myself next to several *sakura* cherry trees that are about to flower. The branches that were awaiting spring's arrival are now white with snow. One branch proudly displays its first blooms.

In the background, I can see the *honden* (main temple building), blurred by the pink blossom and a curtain of falling snow.

The shrine is empty of visitors apart from a solitary couple climbing the stairs toward the honden; they pull on the rope to ring a little bell, and after making a couple of bows toward the interior of the shrine where the *kami* spirits live, they make their wishes in silence.

I shelter under a sakura tree, but it's snowing so hard I'm getting soaked to the skin. I feel the cold in my bones, and I yearn for the arrival of spring.

The distinctive symbol of Shinto shrines is the *torii* gate 鳥居, usually composed of wooden posts painted red. (In point of fact the torii is considered a type of *mon*, though the suffix *mon* doesn't appear in the word.) The torii represents the entry point to the sacred territory inhabited by the *kami* (gods or spirits). When you see this kind of gate you can be pretty sure that you're looking at a Shinto shrine rather than a Buddhist temple, although Buddhist temples do on occasion have torii gates. As torii or mon gates cannot be used as definitive indicators of difference between Buddhist temples and Shinto shrines, you can refer to the chart on page 87 for other key differences.

One thing that torii and mon have in common is that they are elements symbolizing liminality – the threshold between two states, real or metaphysical: life and death, health and sickness, suffering and liberation, or youth and old age, for example.

Matsuri: Festivals

Local festivals, known as *matsuri* 祭り in Japanese are occasions when Shinto and Buddhism are most typically practiced. There are thousands of matsuri, and each one is celebrated in a very different way, but one of the factors common to almost all of them is the carrying of *mikoshi* portable shrines on the shoulders of a crowd of people.

Mikoshi processions and traditional dances are typical festival activities, but sometimes I get the feeling that's the least of it: the important thing is the food, the sake and having a good time with family and friends. During the festival period, *yatai* food stalls are erected in the street or in temple or shrine grounds, with chairs and tables, like sidewalk cafés.

Matsuri and Fertility

"Héctor! I don't care what Wikipedia says! For me mikoshi represent masculinity and shrines femininity," Tago said with a smile, having just gulped down the last of his can of Sapporo.

Tago had spent from six in the morning until three in the afternoon carrying a mikoshi portable

A striking nighttime view of a traditionally decorated stage at a Japanese festival.

shrine on his shoulders with other men from the local area. But far from being tired, the matsuri had given him the energy to talk.

"It says here that during the matsuri people pray to the kami for rain so they'll have good harvests," I answered him with some skepticism.

"Of course," said Tago. "That's why we've carried the mikoshi along all the roads around the rice fields, to fertilize them. But, as I see it, fertility in agriculture, in nature, and in human beings are all pretty much the same thing. Do you remember when we arrived at the shrine with the mikoshi on our shoulders?"

He then took his iPhone from his pocket and showed me a photo he'd taken that morning. The photo showed a huge mikoshi, carried by a crowd of

A striking nighttime view of a traditionally decorated stage at a Japanese festival.

people, being pushed inside a shrine building.

"Right . . . When you look at it like that I suppose there is something sexual about it," I answered, laughing.

"Think about the characters that make up the word shrine," he said to me as he wrote 神宮 (jingu, Shinto shrine) on a piece of paper. "The first character is the one for kami 神 and the second, palace 宮."

"Aha . . ."

"And now let's compare it with the word womb, shikyu 子宮."

"Wow! The literal translation of womb in

Japanese would be palace (宮) of the children (子)," I replied, joining the dots.

"The characters of the word shrine tell us that a shrine represents the female sexual organs," Tago said as he opened another can of Sapporo. "What's more, here's what a shrine looks like from above." He carefully sketched a shrine while I scrolled through my phone. His drawing was quite similar to the plan of a shrine I had already found myself on Google Maps.

"You see, the main temple hall is the womb and the two rooms at the back are the fallopian tubes," said Tago, completely convinced, drawing arrows to emphasize his points.

"Seriously? This is starting to sound like a Dan Brown novel," I replied, skeptically.

"It's true!" Tago said laughing. "Matsuri are acts of sexual reproduction. The men carry mikoshi on their shoulders, moving them up and down rhythmically. When they arrive at the entrance to the shrine they push the mikoshi in, penetrating as far as the 'palace of the children.' There's nothing really strange about what I'm telling you; in the past sex was something sacred and was celebrated communally, not like now, when it's become something taboo," he concluded, raising his voice in excitement.

"You've convinced me," I said, giving him a slap on the shoulder. "The way you put it gives me a rather different perspective on matsuri. When you look at that way, Tago, you've spent the whole day carrying a gigantic sexual member."

Cue lots of laughter.

When he'd finished his second beer we strolled toward the town square where the festivities continued. We bought yakitori grilled chicken at a *yatai* food stall in the street and watched the arrival of various mikoshi belonging to local matsuri groups.

As the sun set behind the Nagano mountains, the Shinto rituals of the official matsuri ceremony drew to a close. The atmosphere was more relaxed

Various nighttime scenes from a traditional local festival taking place in Chiba Prefecture, to the east of Tokyo.

MY TRAVEL TIPS
Attending a Matsuri

More than two hundred thousand *matsuri* festivals take place each year in Japan, meaning that every day there are several in different parts of the country. Bear in mind that when there is a popular matsuri, most local hotels are fully booked months in advance.

Here are the dates of the important matsuri:

Nebuta Matsuri: August 2–7 in Aomori. Said to be the most spectacular matsuri in Japan.

Yuki Matsuri: last week of January and first week of February in Sapporo; exact dates change according to the year.

Sanja Matsuri: third weekend of May in Asakusa, Tokyo.

Tenjin Matsuri: July 24 and 25 in Osaka.

Hakata Gion Yamakasa Matsuri: the main festival of the Kushida Shrine in Fukuoka. From July 10–15.

Gion Matsuri: from the beginning of July and for most of the month in the Gion district of Kyoto and the surrounding neighborhoods.

than in the morning when Shinto rituals had to be strictly followed.

It was lovely to watch people of all ages having a good time together, something that is a rare sight as we go about our daily lives in Japan's big cities. The children were even jumping up onto the floats to play the *taiko* drums!

The Kanamara Matsuri

The Kanamara Matsuri かなまら祭り is a Shinto festival centered on phallus worship. It takes place every year on the first Sunday in April at the Kanayama Shrine in Kawasaki, between Tokyo and Yokohama.

The matsuri is dedicated to the god of fertility and the main procession is a parade of giant phalluses through the streets leading to the shrine.

LEFT The festival of Kanamara is dedicated to the phallus and to fertility in general. The festival is only celebrated once a year, but the metal phallus can be visited any day of the year. The shrine is well signposted from Kawasaki Daishi Station and is less than a minute's walk away.
RIGHT Hats of this style are only found at the Awa Odori festival.

The festival is only celebrated once a year, but the metal phallus can be visited year round.

From Kawasaki Daishi Station the shrine is well signposted and less than a minute's walk away.

The Awa Odori Festival

The Awa Odori 阿波踊り, the Awa Festival of Dance, originates in the city of Tokushima on the island of Shikoku, and is now held in many places. In Tokyo the Awa Odori festival tradition began after the Second World War in the districts of Koenji and Kagurazaka.

I had the good fortune to attend the Awa Odori with a friend who's been going to the festival since the eighties and who was telling me all kinds of details about the very special nature of the dances.

One of the most popular dances is *Odoru aho ni* (Those Who Dance Are Fools). Legend has it that in the year 1586, the daimyo of the province of Awa in present-day Shikoku held a huge party that lasted for several days in his castle in Tokushima. His guests included people from every social class, from peasants to samurai. After drinking copious amounts of sake they started to improvise music and dancing. In their drunken rapture they ended up creating the rhythm, melody and lyrics to the principal tunes still performed to this day:

The festival stems from a legend about a devil that fell in love with a local girl. He became so jealous that he hid inside her vagina and bit off the penis of two different men on their wedding night. The girl asked the village blacksmith to make an iron phallus so that when the devil went to bite it, he would break his teeth. The blacksmith's invention worked. After being used to see off the devil once and for all, the iron phallus became a sacred object in the Kanayama Shrine.

踊る阿呆に	*Odoru aho ni*	Those Who Dance Are Fools
見る阿呆	*Miru aho*	Those Who Watch Are Fools
同じ阿呆なら	*Onaji aho nara*	Everyone Is A Fool
踊らな損、損！	*Odorana son, son!*	Why Not Dance?

After creating these songs and dances they carried on the celebration for days, and began repeating it every year.

Hatsumode

Hatsumode 初詣 is difficult to translate but would be something like "the first visit of the year to the temple or shrine."

I went to hatsumode at Tokyo's Meiji Jingu shrine, where more than three million people go every January. Across the country, a total of around a hundred million Japanese people celebrate the hatsumode tradition. The shrine visit usually takes place on the first, second or third day of the New Year, but it's not a problem if it's a little later.

The standard procedure for hatsumode is to stand in front of the main shrine building, throw a coin into the collection box, clap hands and make a wish. Some temples also offer a special ceremony for which you have to pay; at Meiji Jingu you can

---

MAGICAL DETAILS
Hatsumode Gifts

We attended a special *hatsumode* ceremony at Meiji Jingu shrine. When the ceremony was over we were given a box of gifts that included *omikuji* fortunes, strips of paper predicting your future in matters of love, health, business, etc. If your omikuji predicts bad luck, you can hang it next to a sacred tree and in so doing you will rid yourself of it. If you get good luck, you can keep the omikuji.

In the box there was also a bottle of holy sake, a leaflet giving the history of the shrine, a little box of *anko* sweet red bean paste, as well as a wooden *omamori* amulet.

The Sanja Matsuri

According to legend, on March 18 in the year 628, two brothers were fishing in the Sumida River — in the east of present-day Tokyo — when suddenly they caught something heavy in their nets. It turned out to be a small statue of a human form and they decided to throw it back into the river.

The next day when they went out to fish, the same statue got caught in their net. Again they threw it back into the water. The next day, the same thing happened. On each of these occasions they didn't manage to catch any fish.

When this had happened a number of times, the two brothers decided to take the statue to Hajino Nakatomo, one of the richest and wisest men in the area. On seeing the little statue, Nakatomo told the brothers: "It's the goddess Kannon!"

The three of them decided to build a temple to house the statue. The temple would be dedicated to Kannon, the Buddhist goddess of mercy. And so they founded Senso-ji in Tokyo's Asakusa district, one of the most important Buddhist temples in Japan, which is still visited by millions of people every year.

When the founders of the temple died, the local people built a Shinto shrine called Asakusa Jinja right next to Senso-ji temple, dedicated to the three of them.

Sanja Matsuri 三社祭 literally means "festival of the shrine of the three." In other words it's a festival dedicated to the three founders of Senso-ji temple. It takes place on the third weekend in May in the streets of Asakusa. The processions last for two days and the crucial moment is when the three biggest *mikoshi* portable shrines, dedicated to Hajino Nakatomo and the two fishermen brothers, are brought onto the streets. They each weigh more than a ton and several parts of them are made of pure gold.

The Sanja Matsuri is a great example of the way that the Japanese mix religions and traditions into a potentially confusing blend. The three men founded a Buddhist temple dedicated to Kannon, but when they died they were elevated to the status of *kami* (gods) in a Shinto shrine.

Tokyo's Sanja Matsuri festival is celebrated every year to commemorate the discovery of a Kannon goddess figure by two fishermen brothers in the Sumida River in the year 628.

choose to pay between five thousand and fifty thousand yen depending on the level of protection and good luck you want. Many temples and shrines are a real business and they don't try to hide it; I was even given the option of paying by credit card for the special hatsumode ceremony I attended.

Depending on what you pay, at the end of the ceremony they give you an amulet called an *omamori* お守り (lit., guardian) the size of which can vary from large to small. You have to take it home and place it in a conspicuous spot so that it will protect you throughout the year. When you do hatsumode the following year, you have to return your omamori to the same shrine or temple you got it from, where it will be burned at the base of a sacred tree.

The special hatsumode ceremony we attended at Meiji Jingu shrine started with a drink of sake before we entered the room where the ceremony was held. We knelt on tatami mats, which reminded me of the way we used to sit at the start of the judo classes I went to when I was a child in Spain.

The priest leading the ceremony stood facing the altar and attendants started to play *taiko* drums. Then we bowed our heads and they proceeded to "purify" us with s*akaki* evergreen branches, waving them over our heads.

Millions of Japanese celebrate the *hatsumode* tradition at temples and shrines across the country. People can buy *omikuji* paper scrolls with fortunes written on them. Sake producers in pay to have their products displayed on a shrine altar to bring them good business in the coming year.

The priest then sat with his back to us, facing the altar where the *kami* (gods or spirits) are said to reside, and started to speak in ancient Japanese. He asked the kami to grant us good health, luck, happiness and wealth for the coming year.

After two minutes of making these wishes, he recited out loud the names of all those present. This took quite a while, since there were about a hundred people in the room.

The fact that the priest didn't address the congregation in the name of God, as happens in other traditions, but rather spoke to the kami to make wishes on our behalf, struck me as the oddest part of the experience. It's a subtle but important difference that can help us understand not only Shinto but Asian religions in general.

Shinto in Ghibli's *Spirited Away*

Spirited Away is one of those few movies which never fails to surprise me no matter how many times I watch it. It can be read and interpreted from many different points of view: it's an adventure movie that is brimming with important life lessons; the heroine is a little girl; it takes you to the heart of Japanese culture and mythology; it's a critique of the greed of Japanese capitalism in the 1980s; it's a love story . . .

Spirited Away can be enjoyed as a simple fairy tale, but it also can be interpreted as an exploration of how our greedy and corrupt modern societies have lost touch with the elements considered important by the Shinto religion, particularly our connection with nature. The narrative can be considered a metaphor for how a more spiritual life can help us reconnect to nature, one of the core tenets of Shinto.

The narrative of the movie *Spirited Away* centers on a girl called Chihiro, who, with her parents, enters a mysterious world filled with *kami* gods and spirits. Upon entering this parallel world, her parents are overcome by gluttony as they greedily devour food at a restaurant stall and they end up turning into pigs. Chihiro comes to the realization that even the world of the spirits has been overtaken by greed.

Magical Details in *Spirited Away*

- **Kaonashi** is the name of a faceless spirit that appears in the movie. The blank face of this character is inspired by the actors' masks in traditional Japanese Noh theater.

- **Konpeito** is the name for the colorful Japanese candy eaten by the soot sprites in the movie.

- **Old fashioned train tickets** are given to protagonist Chihiro by Kamaji, the man who works at the hot spring. They are an old type of ticket that are barely used now, but they are actually still sold in Japan, in packs of eleven.

- **Ajisai** is the Japanese name for hydrangeas, which feature in the movie. Hydrangeas flower in Japan from the last week of June to the first week of July.

- **Vertical society** is a term that can be used to describe the way in which the workers are organized at the hot spring bath house where Chihiro works. This mirrors the feudal hierarchical structures I cover in chapter 2.

The character Kaonashi has a face inspired by traditional Noh theater masks. The soot sprites hold traditional Japanese candy, called *konpeito*.

Earlier I mentioned that *Spirited Away* takes you to the heart of Japanese culture. For example, the influence of the ancient Japanese legend of Izanagi and Izanami can be clearly seen. The story goes that the goddess Izanami, after creating Japan with the god Izanagi, died after giving birth to the god of fire, Kagutsuchi. Izanagi would not accept the death of his wife and decided to journey to the underworld to try to bring her back with him to the world of the living.

He managed to find her, but Izanami said to him: "I have eaten so many delicacies in this realm that it would be difficult to go back; you can go without me." Much to his regret, Izanagi had to return to the world of the living, leaving his wife behind. Later they would be reunited as the "wedded rocks" known as Meoto Iwa in Mie Prefecture (see page 178).

This is one of many Japanese legends in which consuming something produced in another world has adverse effects. The moral of the story is that we should eat in moderation. The gluttony and avarice of Chihiro's parents leads them to stuffing themselves at a free food stall and they end up as pigs, which hinders their return to the world of the living.

By contrast, Chihiro's heart is so pure that she decides to eat nothing, but this strategy doesn't seem to work either, as she begins to fade away. Fortunately at that moment she meets the river spirit Haku, who saves her life by giving her rice to eat.

The influence of Shinto can be seen elsewhere in *Spirited Away.* Shinto advocates the purity and kindness of human beings and of living creatures in general. When someone carries out a malevolent deed it's because they have been taken over by evil spirits.

In *Spirited Away,* all the characters can be seen to evolve. The protagonist, Chihiro, goes from being a little girl to having to work as though she were just another grown-up. She must lose her innocence working in the service of greedy, treacherous gods, with coworkers like the spirit Kaonashi (whose

---

MY TRAVEL TIPS

Buying Tickets for the Ghibli Museum

The Ghibli Museum is the mecca for any fan of movies from the Japanese animation company Studio Ghibli. And even if you don't consider yourself a Ghibli fan, it's still an excellent place to spend a few hours, especially if you're traveling with children.

The museum is close to Mitaka Station, about twenty minutes from the center of Tokyo by Chuo Line train from Shinjuku Station. The important thing to remember is that you won't be able to buy tickets at the museum: they have to be bought in advance.

The best options for buying tickets

- **Via a specialized travel agent in Japan** You can buy tickets up to four months in advance.

- **At ticket machines in Lawson convenience stores** This is a good option if you can read Japanese. Lawson also has an English-language page on its website where tickets can be bought outside Japan: l-tike.com/st1/ghibli-en/sitetop. If you have a question or a problem, Lawson also has an email address for English-language queries: ghibli@ent.lawson.co.jp

Extra information

- The museum is usually closed on Tuesdays.
- There are four guided tours daily, at 10 a.m., noon, 2 p.m. and 4 p.m.

HOW TO GET THERE

From Shinjuku Station take the JR Chuo Line (destination Takao). Make sure you get on a train which is stopping at Mitaka (some of the express trains will pass through without stopping). The train journey takes about twenty minutes. At Mitaka Station take the south exit. The Ghibli Museum is well signposted from there.

name literally means "No Face") who gradually become possessed by greed, corruption and avarice.

Director Hayao Miyazaki uses the movie to praise the purity of childlike values and criticize the corruption of the world of adults.

Another theme in *Spirited Away* is the importance of names. The Japanese title of the movie is *Sen to Chihiro no kamikakushi* 千と千尋の神隠し. A more literal translation would be "The mysterious disappearance of the spirits of Sen and Chihiro."

Kamikakushi 神隠し is almost impossible to translate accurately; the first character 神 means *kami*, spirits or gods; and the second character 隠し means *kakushi*, hide. Both characters together take on the meaning of "mysterious disappearance" or "spirited away," but the movie is not the story of a disappearance, it's rather a journey to the great beyond in order to rediscover oneself. *Sen to Chihiro* 千と千尋 is the most important part of the title since it's one of the main themes of the movie. The characters of Chihiro 千尋 mean 千 *chi* "thousand" and 尋 *hiro*, to search for.

In the part of the movie when Yubaba the witch steals Chihiro's name, she magically takes away the second character 尋, leaving only 千 (which is pronounced *sen* when it stands alone). When

Chihiro thus ends up being turned into Sen by Yubaba, she is forced a step further into the world of the spirits where she will have to face many trials before being able to return with her parents to the real world.

All cultures of the world place great importance on proper names. In the European tradition there are stories like *Rapunzel* by the Brothers Grimm, in which one of the principal themes is the significance of proper names.

In the case of Japan, not only is the pronunciation of a name important, but also the characters used to write a name and their meaning. It is believed that the written characters of a person's name convey part of the spirit of that person. A device often seen in Japanese movies and novels is the loss of a name, through theft, forgetting, or even never using a character's name at all, as seen in several of the works of Haruki Murakami.

He who knows a person's name,
Holds that person's life in his hands.
– Ursula K. Le Guin

As well as themes relating to philosophical issues such as Shinto, there are many other enjoyable reflections of life in Japan in *Spirited Away*. For

many viewers, the movie might be a first introduction to the widespread phenomenon of *onsen* hot-spring bathing. Protagonist Chihiro ends up working in a hot-springs bathhouse for the evil witch Yubaba, as punishment for her parents' gluttony. This element of the movie is widely regarded as a metaphor for prostitution.

The movie also deals with more serious, universal issues, such as pollution. One of the kami in the movie is possessed by an evil spirit and turns into a foul monster that nobody is brave enough to meet. It is Chihiro who understands that it's not his fault he's become what he is, it is because he is the kami of a polluted river.

In Japan, rivers are often polluted, and one of the major pollutants is discarded bicycles. Because bicycles are licensed in Japan, it's difficult to get rid of them without paying a fee, so the easiest and cheapest way to dispose of a bicycle that is no longer wanted is to throw it into a river. The first thing that Chihiro takes from the mouth of the polluted kami is a bicycle.

Pollution is also one of the main themes of the movie *Ponyo*, also by Miyazaki.

Satoyama and the Gods of Nature

One of the functions of Shinto shrines is to make it easier for the kami to "descend" to the areas where people live and help them with their harvests. You will typically see Shinto shrines in the border zone between forested mountains and cultivated fields. This border zone is called *satoyama* 里山 (里 meaning "arable land," " area with life"; 山 meaning "mountain"). The word is also used to describe the type of ecosystem that forms in these types of places.

For an area to be considered satoyama it must be surrounded by rice fields, pools and ponds, irrigation channels and forest. Satoyama land is fertile, and although the rice fields may be small in area, they are usually productive.

Satoyama implies making the most of the land: for example, the grass at the edge of the forest is used to feed animals, the ponds are used for irrigation but also for fish-farming, and the leaves that fall from the trees are used for fertilizer.

We can explain the phenomenon of satoyama through the Prism of the Islands of Few Resources (see chapter 2). As Japan's scarce arable land has to support a population of 127 million people, it's important to make the most of every resource, no matter how tiny.

Yunnan in China, Bali and the Philippines are some of the places with rice fields which are most visited by tourists. In Japan they're not so spectacular, but you can also see some terraced hillsides. We found these fields in the south of Chiba.

Irrigation channels are important. If someone in a rice field higher up contaminates the water with a chemical product, it affects the people with rice fields lower down, especially in the villages, which tend to be in the lowest lying areas. The upkeep of the whole of the rice-growing area is the responsibility of the community; it's like looking after a huge garden.

"Recently there haven't been enough people in the village to look after the area where the bamboo is practically invading the road," a villager called Akira, from Kamogawa in Chiba Prefecture, told me with a sigh. "Everyone leaves for Tokyo and they never come back; it's more and more difficult to maintain the harmony of the satoyama here . . ."

I've spent several holidays surrounded by Japanese nature. One of the best things is waking up to the lovely murmur of the bamboo forests as the breeze comes down the mountains into the valleys. The worst thing is the spiders.

Traveling through Japan you can easily identify satoyama areas; you'll see them as soon as you leave Narita Airport on the train. If you haven't been to Japan, watch Ghibli movies like *My Neighbor Totoro*, whose scenes are inspired by the satoyama of Saitama Prefecture.

In the summer of 2014 I made my first visit to a rice-growing region in Chiba Prefecture, near Tokyo, which I fell in love with. It wasn't just the place, it was also the new friends I made there, prompting me to return several times to breathe the Japanese country air.

After a time the local people offered me membership of an association of rice-field owners. My first reaction was to reject the offer: it sounded like something that might be an extra burden in my life. But having thought it over for a few days I remembered one of the wisest pieces of advice my friend Rodrigo gave me: "In life you have to invest in stories."

This business of the rice fields in Chiba sounded like an ideal situation for "investing in stories," so I ended up accepting. For a few months it was a bit annoying having to read and sign contracts, transfer money to association

bank accounts, read regulations about the maintenance of rice fields, speak to other members on
the phone . . . It was like having to deal with one of
those secret societies in a Haruki Murakami
novel. But in the end I not only became a member,
they also gave me a seat on the board of directors.

Although I had to invest a considerable
amount of time in the association, I did harvest a
lot of stories. There was the time when a group of
about twenty friends, along with a hundred or so
of the local villagers, got together and planted
rice by hand. We methodically placed the shoots
one by one in perfect alignment using string so as
not to lose the symmetry: the shoots have to be
more or less the same distance apart. We over-
came our fear of sinking in the mud, of walking
without falling into the water and of plunging our
hands into the mud while frogs crawled up our
arms. We learned to plant the rice seedlings using
only two fingers just like the farm workers in an
Akira Kurosawa movie.

When we'd finished, we were interviewed on
Chiba local radio and they invited us to a party
with at least a hundred farmers, where the food
was paid for by the local council. As a member of
the board of the regional rice-field association I
had get up onto the platform and thank everyone
for their hard work planting rice.

Planting rice in the traditional way made me
appreciate the importance of Japanese agriculture and its influence on village culture. As
participants in rice planting we had to coordinate and work collectively to line up the shoots as
straight as possible. It's important for the
community to work in unison and for everyone to
collaborate to get the best harvest.

The farmers explained to me that each field is
the property of one of the farmers from the area;
you don't only have to work in your own rice field,
you also have to help out with the planting and
maintenance of neighboring plots. The misfortune of a bad harvest for your neighbor one year

could well be your misfortune the next. If one
person doesn't look after their field it can affect
the rest. For example, the fields are terraced, so
the irrigation of one field affects the irrigation of
neighboring plots. It is therefore important that
the farmers coordinate with each other to avoid
problems and maximize rice production, agree-
ing for example not to use chemical products to
eliminate weeds. One farmer, who produces
organic rice, explained to me that he wants to
grow rice free of pesticides, but that he can't do
this if the owner of the neighboring paddy is
using them.

Again, this fits in with the group mentality
that is prominent in Japan, as neighboring rice
field owners help each other and take decisions
collectively. There can also be problems, for
example if there's someone in the group who
doesn't agree with the way everyone else is
thinking and working. The group mentality can
be a source of social pressure, forcing you to
choose between going along with the ways of the
group or risk becoming an outcast.

"*Even in a world of pain and suffering,
Flowers keep on blooming.*"

—Kobayashi Issa

CHAPTER 7
The Dark Side of Japan

Not everything in Japan is beautiful, perfect and magical: the country also has a less favorable side. During my first few years here I didn't want to focus on the negative, but the moment has arrived to talk about what I've learned.

This chapter was inspired by various conversations that my friend Rodrigo and I had on camera on our YouTube channel *The Geek and the Friki* talking about "dark Japan." The theme of "dark Japan" has also been dealt with by Spanish author Marc Bernabé in his recent book *Japón* (Japan).

I write this with maximum respect to Japan and the Japanese people, whom I admire and care about greatly. I'm blaming nobody; this is just a rather more critical look at certain aspects of this society that I consider to be slightly less than ideal.

A Low Crime Rate

Having said that, I can't avoid starting with the positive. Japan has one of the lowest crime rates in the world. Tokyo is considered the safest of the world's large cities. In fact, a common argument among Japanese politicians is whether they need to reduce the size of the police force, given that there isn't enough crime to keep the police busy.

One of the main reasons why people feel comfortable in Japan is because it's so safe. You can leave your phone or computer on your café table while you go to the bathroom, and there's nothing to fear when walking through the

A pianist performs at the seventieth birthday party of photographer Nobuyoshi Araki, to which I was lucky enough to be invited.

streets of big cities at night, for example.

I could tell dozens of stories of friends and relatives who've lost something — a suitcase, a computer, even a wallet full of money — which they've almost always had returned to them.

One curious phenomenon of the last few years is the number of crimes committed by the over sixties. Why? It turns out the social security systems are so inadequate that once Japanese people reach retirement age many of them have insufficient money to look after themselves. Desperation forces them to steal food from supermarkets and some of them reoffend deliberately because they want to go to jail, where they'll be looked after. Some Japanese prisons are turning into old people's homes, where they're having to employ nurses as well as prison warders to take care of the elderly.

The Yakuza

Despite occupying one of the top spots in lists of countries with low crime rates, it's clear that there is activity on the fringes of the law that many prefer to ignore.

The yakuza have the "honor" of being one of the largest criminal organizations in the world. Their area of expertise is taking advantage of legal loopholes in order to launder money. To survive as an organization they use blackmail, extortion, con tricks and virtually undetectable fraud. They carry

An arguably suspicious meeting near Shinjuku Station. Despite Japan's low crime rate, it's obvious that there is activity on the fringes of the law that society prefers to ignore.

out their business at the margins of the law; the authorities don't usually get involved. By the same token, the yakuza themselves don't interfere with citizens who are not part of their organization.

When I've come across yakuza they've treated me well. One of them told me I'd dropped my wallet in the street. One paid for my dinner; he was sitting at the next table in a restaurant and after chatting at great length, he said goodbye, footing the bill for our meal when he left.

But there was a particular incident that stands out. I was taking photos with my friend Javi in Shinjuku's entertainment district of Kabukicho. We took a photo of a seemingly empty building with frosted windows, in which, unbeknown to us, a yakuza meeting was taking place. One of them saw us and came out into the street to tell us to get the hell out of there. When tried to placate him, explaining that I would delete the photos he said: "I don't care about the photos, get out of here before my bosses find out what you've been up to."

It's like there's an unwritten agreement. The

police leave the yakuza in peace and in exchange for this, the yakuza treat regular citizens well. This has brought about a strange equilibrium that nobody seems to want to disrupt.

Madogiwa: Ostracism

The word *madogiwa* literally means "next to the window," and is used to label company employees who aren't assigned any important work to do and who are ignored. The phenomenon is something that seemed unreal, even funny, when I first read about it. Etched on my mind is the novel *Fear and Trembling* by Amélie Nothomb, the story of a young Belgian woman who went from having an enviable professional career to having to clean the company bathroom. At the time I had no idea that I would be a victim of madogiwa myself; the only good thing about the story I'm about to tell you is that I didn't end up having to clean the bathroom.

Here is a diary entry of mine, a few years ago:

> *This week they gave me a salary cut and moved me to a seat next to the window near a couple of photocopiers. Around me, all the other desks are empty except those of three other colleagues from my own team who've also been downgraded.*
>
> *All the projects I was responsible for have been taken away from me and transferred to other departments; I find myself with no work to do. I've spent the day surfing the web and chatting online with friends to raise my spirits. I send my bosses the occasional email with suggestions for new projects but they don't answer. I've ended up scrolling through job search websites to see if I can find something new.*

Madogiwa is a technique to get people to leave the company without having to get rid of them directly. In Japan, firing employees is looked down upon.

What was the main reason I was banished to the seat by the window?

It turns out that I committed the mistake of *jikadanpan* (talking to someone directly) when I communicated my discontent with my immediate bosses to the chairman of the company.

This had happened one day when I was in the company cafeteria with two coworkers and the chairman came up to us to say hello. Besides talking about the cold weather that Tokyo was having as autumn arrived, he also asked, "How's everything in your department since your new bosses arrived?"

A woman waits for her date at Shibuya Station.

"Fine," we mumbled, although things weren't really fine at all. So I added, "There's maybe a communication problem in our department." The chairman listened with interest and didn't seem annoyed with me in the least, quite the opposite in fact. He told me I'd done the right thing by telling him about the problem and added that he was very pleased with my work of late, and that I should carry on doing what I was doing.

The conversation lasted barely five minutes and ended with lots of laughter. But it seems that the new bosses in our department ended up being reprimanded, and I was to blame.

About an hour or so later, all the workers in my team, including those of us who'd been in the cafeteria talking to the chairman, received an email with the title "Special Meeting," The email was short, only saying, "From three o'clock onward, come one by one into meeting room C." No further details were given.

I watched all my colleagues go in to the meeting room and come out again barely a minute later. One of them tipped me off, whispering, "They're after you." Finally, when it was my turn I entered that soulless room; there was so much tension in the air I felt as though I was in an interrogation cell in an American detective movie.

Three big shots with serious faces were sitting in front of me. One of them, who had a singsong voice, said to me: "It was you who spoke to the chairman this morning, wasn't it?" I felt I had nothing to hide, so I said yes.

Staring at me furiously he went on: "And what did you say to him?" Still not really understanding what was going on, and wondering what it was that could have caused such an upheaval, I told them everything in great detail. They stopped me as soon as I told them that I'd said to the chairman that there was a communication problem.

"Do you really think we have a communication problem?" said the man with the singsong voice, which was now tinged with a mixture of contempt and hatred. The other two bosses, arms folded, nodded their heads as though to underline his question.

The absurdity and irony of the situation were

bewildering; they were interrogating me on my own in a meeting room, with nobody else allowed to enter, and they were asking me if we had a communication problem.

Up to this point I'd stayed calm, but the rest of the interrogation almost ended up in a fight. "Never speak to the chairman again without our permission" they said. "I'm free to speak to whoever I please, whenever I want," I answered. "You are in no position to decide if we have problems or not! You are a traitor!" said the boss sitting on the right, raising his voice on the word "traitor."

They hadn't liked it one little bit that I had complained directly to the chairman without having said anything to them. This in itself wasn't completely correct: for months, a small group of us, not just me, had been vocal in pointing out things we thought should be changed, but our voices had been ignored. But my explanation really didn't matter — what had offended them most was the fact that I'd spoken directly to the chairman, violating the strict Japanese protocol which says you have follow the chain of command as though you were part of a military organization. I had broken with the long-held traditions of the Prism of Feudal Structures (see chapter 2).

After having been made to feel like a criminal, I walked out of the room scared to speak to anyone else and with the decision in my heart that I had to get out of the company as soon as I could, whatever the cost. In retrospect, the strange thing is that the chairman at no point told them that I'd been the one who had spoken out. It seems that he simply told them that he'd heard rumors from the engineering team that we should improve communication within the company — exactly as had been discussed in our conversation in the cafeteria. The management must have decided that I was the culprit after questioning all members of the engineering team individually.

A salaryman makes his way to the train station.

That same day, the three bosses who'd interrogated me came to see me, told me to put all my things in a box and moved me across to a desk next the window and the photocopiers. I also received several emails in which I was told that I'd been removed from all projects and that my salary was being cut.

The next day, when I arrived at work, there was nothing for me to do.

After this happened, I left the company, along with the several other coworkers who had also been downgraded. Feeling betrayed, I decided I would never work in a Japanese company again.

Being young, it was easy for me to find another job, but for people who end up as madogiwa at the age of fifty or fifty-five it's very difficult to find a new job, and they just have to put up with sitting in front of a computer screen until retirement day arrives.

I once met a fifty-eight-year-old madogiwa who spent all day looking at pictures of tigers on his computer. I also saw him sometimes planning his weekend trips, all of them to zoos to see tigers. Nobody around him knew what his job was; the only thing we knew about him was that he liked tigers.

A Shared Lie: Honne and Tatemae

Besides defying the structures imposed by the Prism of Feudal Structures, another of the reasons why I was attacked in such a way was because I told the truth (*honne*). We employees knew that there was a communication problem in the company, but nobody dared to say it out loud; they stayed silent because they feel bound by honne's opposite: *tatemae*.

Honne could be defined as the desires, opinions and true thoughts which each individual has. Tatemae refers to how we adjust our opinions to fit with our social obligations and the thinking of society in general.

Dark and dirty alleyways are still common in the city centers of Tokyo and Osaka.

In most aspects of everyday life, Japanese people tend to observer tatemae, in other words they hide their true feelings. But if for example they're having a drink with friends perhaps they'll switch to honne in order to express how they really feel.

The good thing about tatemae is that it helps to ensure that from one day to the next, business and social relationships between colleagues at work proceed without conflict. It's a type of lubricant to keep the peace in society and it works well in brief interactions. But when it's misused, especially over longer periods of time, tatemae can end up turning into a shared lie, and the consequences can be awful.

Some foreigners who've just arrived in Japan and who don't take well to tatemae, categorize it as hypocrisy or outright lying; I prefer to call it "embellishing the truth."

In certain contexts it's easy to spot the tatemae if both parties understand the real truth beneath the spin. In other cultures we occasionally have tatemae. For instance, when we go to buy a car from a dealer, we know that the salesperson is playing the role of salesperson and we the role of customers.

Tatemae could be defined as how we adjust our opinions to fit the thinking of those around us. It allows relationships between coworkers to proceed without conflict.

As customers we have to be able to read between the lines of what we're being told; if not, we'd end up buying the first car we were offered. The salesperson also knows we're not going to buy the first car.

To live comfortably in Japan, you have learn how to detect what's being communicated beneath the surface of a conversation. It's not enough to know how to handle yourself in a car dealership; in practically every situation you come across, tatemae comes into play.

In negotiations in Japan, both sides will maintain the tatemae as long as possible, but in the end, they'll put everything in the table. If the tatemae is, let's say, "synchronized" on both sides, in other words if both parties have more or less the same conditions in mind, the agreement will be signed. On the other hand if that's not the case, negotiations will fall through. In other cultures we're more

direct from the start; in this way we reach agreement (or disagreement) more quickly.

I marvel at the Japanese ability to "synchronize" themselves when it comes to tatemae. It is not difficult to see that tatemae is fundamental for maintaining *wa*, peace and harmony, and avoiding conflict. But appearances can be deceptive.

If a little fib arises in a tatemae situation but then begins to spread among a group of people, it can end up becoming a very large shared lie. Everyone knows there's something fishy going on but they choose to look the other way, and nobody dares tell the truth.

These lies, which are shared across Japanese society, generally never come to light, but when they do, they erupt spectacularly, often in the form of political and business corruption scandals in which many heads roll. Normally there's not just one person to blame; responsibility is shared by those who kept the lie going.

The balance between honne and tatemae maintains harmony, but an excess of tatemae can lead to a fear of telling the truth.

Like all countries, Japan has its good and bad. Most Japanese people will at some point come up against the mysterious unwritten rules imposed by their society.

Ijime: Bullying

Ijime can be translated as bullying, an increasingly serious problem in schools across the world. In this section I'm going to try to explain the peculiarities of Japanese bullying, a phenomenon that extends beyond schools to the world of business, leading to ostracism and marginalization.

Let's start with schools. According to studies by Mitsuru Taki at the National Institute of Education Research, the majority of bullying in Japanese schools occurs between children of the same age, whereas in other parts of the world victims tend to be younger than their bullies. Another characteristic of Japanese school bullying, according to Taki's findings, is that the harassment is more psychological than physical, and as such is more difficult for adults to detect and prevent.

The techniques favored by Japanese children to harass others are to ignore, to exclude, to insult,

tants suffer, the funnier it is. But what you see on *Takeshi's Castle* is mild compared to other shows that haven't made it outside Japan.

School bullying is minimized to an extent by the fact that Japanese students all wear uniforms, and carry the same style of bag. The aim is that nobody stands out from the crowd or draws attention to themselves.

Deru kui wa utareru
出る杭は打たれる
The stake that sticks up gets hammered down

But as everywhere, people want to assert their individuality. Students put badges or accessories on their bags or sometimes wear colored socks or other insignia to express their identities.

As for the school bullies, the collectivist spirit (discussed in chapter 4) allows them to feel less responsibility if they are in the bullying group, so that they don't believe they're doing anything wrong. These are feelings that are engendered from a young age.

As there is little to gain from reporting bullying, it is ignored by those who witness it. Even teachers may choose to say nothing; there have even been cases where the teachers themselves were making fun of those who were being harassed.

The problem came to national attention when there were several recent incidents of children who had suffered ijime and went on to commit suicide. After teachers denied all knowledge of the bullying and were later proved to have lied, the law was changed to make everyone responsible — including those passively involved. Since the introduction of the new law, systems have been put in place to encourage children to report bullying incidents.

and to carry out secret beatings. Excluding and ignoring are the most endemic forms of bullying and are the ones that also extend into the business world and society in general.

Because society tends to turn its back on bullying, there are many people who end up suffering psychological disorders, and this leads to extreme behavior such as *hikikomori* (shutting yourself indoors) or even suicide. At the time of writing this book in 2020, the suicide rate among the Japanese population is one of the highest in the world, though fortunately it has been coming down little by little since the year 2005.

The culture of ijime is so entrenched and penetrates so many aspects of Japanese life that people almost take it for granted. For example, it's right there on television. One of the fundamentals of Japanese comedy and variety shows is the ridiculing, humiliation and even brutal physical assault of people in front of the cameras. In the TV program *Takeshi's Castle* (*MXC* in the US), which has become famous overseas, the more the contes-

LEFT Bullying is a problem in the Japanese school system, leading to marginalization and isolation.
RIGHT Each school has an official uniform; it's possible to tell which school students belong to through their uniforms.

For example, schools have introduced mailboxes for children to be able to write anonymously to teachers. As a result, cases have been falling from year to year and the problem of ijime is becoming less and less significant.

Uwaki: Infidelity

Suezen kuwanu wa otoko no haji
据え膳食わぬは男の恥
It's a shame for a man not to eat a feast placed before him
                    — popular Japanese saying

Hito no fuko wa mitsu no aji
ひとの不幸は蜜の味
The misfortune of others tastes like honey
                    — popular Japanese saying

The word for infidelity in Japanese is *uwaki* 浮気. In Japan and other parts of Asia infidelity is a more commonly and morally accepted phenomenon than in the West.

"I just can't understand why there are so many extramarital affairs in this country," says my friend who runs a psychotherapy practice in Shibuya. "A large proportion of the people who come to me for help have problems related to infidelity."

"Are there more men or women who are unfaithful?" I ask out of curiosity.

She stops to think for a moment and finally answers, undecided: "Most of my clients are women, so it's hard to say. About equal, maybe, I guess . . ."

Later, I check the statistics in a survey from the Ministry of Health, Labor and Welfare: Japanese men are twice as unfaithful as Japanese women.

Cheating, in general terms, is not looked upon kindly in Japan, but it's not as taboo as it is in other countries. I suspect — and this is a hypothesis, not a theory — that the reason it's so widespread is because guilt is not a such a factor here. In cultures influenced by Christianity we have the direct commandment:

"Thou shall not commit adultery." (Exodus 20:14; Deuteronomy 5:18; Corinthians 6:9).

Similar commandments exist in Judaism and Islam. By contrast in Japan, and also in Asia generally, there is no religious commandment that says that cheating on your husband or wife is in itself a bad thing. This leads to a dual morality that allows people to act in very different ways in public and in private.

Some people – not all – think like this:

"When nobody's looking I can do what I like."

"The only problem is getting caught (*Barenakya ii* バレなきゃいい) – that would be so embarrassing."

The latter is a set expression used to justify infidelity. A survey of thousands of Tokyo women between the ages of eighteen and sixty asked if they would ever cheat on their partners. The results were as follows:

55.25 percent of the women answered that if they could be sure of not getting caught they would have no problem having an affair.

4.5 percent answered that they would do it despite the risk of getting caught.

The rest answered that they would never cheat on their partners.

The moral logic centers on whether others find out or not, and on the feeling of shame. A Westerner might give more thought to the feeling of guilt than to the feeling of shame before cheating on a partner. Shame can be avoided if nobody finds out, while guilt isn't something you can get rid of easily.

"I feel lonely," Aya says to her best friend. "My boyfriend is so busy with work I only see him a couple of times a month."

"Why don't you get yourself an extra boyfriend?" her friend replies.

Sometimes infidelity is a shared lie; the husband knows his wife is sleeping with another man and she knows he's sleeping with other women, but they stay married to keep the family and kids together and so on. "My husband cheats on me but I put up with it for the children," says the wife.

But don't go getting the idea that Japan is a cheater's paradise either. If you're thinking of coming here to let your hair down, perhaps the

Shop signs in Kabukicho, Shinjuku's red-light district. The red and yellow sign on the right is advertising a peep show.

story of Sada Abe will cool your ardor. Abe was a former geisha and prostitute who, in 1935, started work as an apprentice in a restaurant owned by Kichizo Ishida, a married man with a reputation as a womanizer. One night when Abe was working late, Ishida kissed her and they began an affair.

Abe fell passionately in love with Ishida and the thought of him being married began to make her feel very jealous. One night, while they were making love, Abe strangled and killed him. When he was dead, she cut off his penis and put it in the inside pocket of her kimono. She had Ishida's penis with her until she was arrested by the authorities.

Ishida's penis was put on display in the University of Tokyo Medical Pathology Museum until just after the Second World War, when it suddenly and inexplicably disappeared.

When questioned at the police station, Sada Abe confessed: "I loved him so much that I wanted him all for myself. But since we weren't married, he could be loved by other women—but only as long as he was alive. I knew that if I killed him no other woman would ever touch him again, and that's why I did it."

Conclusion

I've left much unsaid. Overwork and stress are at epidemic levels in Japan's big cities. As a result, alcohol abuse and a multitude of mental illnesses are affecting more and more people. Suicide is another widespread problem that also needs to be addressed.

The types of behavior we've been analyzing in this chapter are the consequence of multiple factors, but one of the most salient is the considerable social pressure that is placed on individuals to conform to societal norms. This pressure to be accepted by others can often lead to extreme forms of behavior.

The solutions to the problems associated with this "shady" aspect of Japanese life are not one-dimensional; it's easy to blame individuals for what you perceive to be wrong when you don't fully understand the perspective through which they see things.

Having said that, and having developed a certain amount of moral flexibility after living in Japan for so long, I'm still taken aback when I find out that a person I admire acts differently when nobody's watching.

A display in a sex shop in Shibuya. Not everything in Japan is beautiful and magical. The country also has a dark side.

"Mount Fuji watches over the sea of concrete, the sunset bathes the city in its red glow . . . Oh, Tokyo . . . oh!"

CHAPTER 8
The Magic of Tokyo

Tokyo, and the urban region around it which forms the Greater Tokyo area, is a sort of gigantic living being whose tentacles extend from the Pacific coast to the mountains of Nikko in the north, and to Tanzawa and Okutama to the west. It's a shapeless amoeba that stretches as far as it's possible to build.

In this megalopolis the lives of forty million people from all over the world are concentrated, forming a blend of cultures, ideas and fashions. I suspect that one of the main reasons I've spent so long in Japan is because I love Tokyo. It wouldn't be the same if I'd had to live in some village in the *inaka* (countryside or rural area).

This love of Tokyo originates perhaps in the sweet recollection of my first few years here when, maybe for the first time in my life, I tasted the freedom to be able to do whatever I wanted, rather than what I was supposed to do.

Tokyo has never judged me; it gives me the freedom to express myself and to be myself. It allows me to choose my own road and at the same time it is constantly transforming me.

I suspect this is not something I'm alone in feeling; I think it's one of the reasons why the districts of Harajuku, Shibuya and Akihabara are crucibles of innovation. Young people dress, dance and sing without fear of being judged: thanks to this freedom, fashions emerge which spread throughout Asia and even across the world.

In Tokyo your choices are so numerous that you have an almost infinite number of roads to follow.

Mount Fuji can sometimes be glimpsed from Tokyo at sunset from a high floor in a west-facing building, especially in winter.

The problem is deciding from among so many possibilities: there are hundreds of museums and galleries; a multitude of theme parks; musicians from all over the world give concerts practically every weekend; there are dozens of universities, thousands of clubs and private schools where you can learn almost everything imaginable; enormous green spaces in practically every neighborhood . . .

There's not just an accumulation of quantity, but also a concentration of quality. Restaurant guides say that some of the best restaurants in the world can be found in Tokyo.

And on top of all that, Tokyo is such a vast city that you can be anonymous and just disappear whenever you want.

Tokyo is also a space shuttle, a transit area, where people get on board for a while and then get off. I've met a lot of people who were only here for a few months or years and ended up leaving.

A while back my friend Nando came to Tokyo for a few days for the first time and sent me a message:

"Today we're visiting Akihabara! I'm telling you so you can bear this in mind when you're planning the walk we're going to do at the weekend . . ."

To which I answered:

"OK, we won't go to Akihabara at the weekend. All the same, I've been here for fifteen years and I have to say I still don't know more than 10 percent of Tokyo."

Nando couldn't believe it.

But despite the fact that I still feel there is so much about this city that I don't know, I'm going to share with you in this chapter a list of fifty things that have captivated me so far. Getting lost in Tokyo's streets — which are so numerous that I couldn't get to know them all in several lifetimes — is one of my hobbies. This chapter is about Tokyo because it's the place I know best, but the majority of these observations could be applied to other Japanese cities.

For me Tokyo is a hypnotic mystery and will forever be so.

50 Things I Love About Tokyo

[1] Side Streets

Walking aimlessly until you feel lost is a fascinating experience. To succeed in getting lost, the best strategy is to get away from the train station and into the side streets.

I love the little winding streets of Tokyo. Sometimes they're so narrow that even though traffic is allowed cars don't dare go into them. When the traffic disappears, Tokyo is transformed into a territory dominated by alley cats, pedestrians and *mamachari* (bicycles with baskets at the front for carrying shopping).

Walking around these streets is entertaining because you don't know what you're going to find around the next corner. You might come across a skyscraper, a market garden growing tomatoes and *goya* (a bitter vegetable native to Okinawa), or several cats having an afternoon nap in the doorway of a house that could just as easily be in a mountain village as in the center of Tokyo.

In the chapter on architecture in my earlier book *A Geek in Japan*, I talk in more detail about the fractal nature of this city. Symmetry is a constant theme, with certain standard patterns that seem to repeat themselves, but there are tiny variations here and there, giving a surprise factor that will please any flaneur.

How do you find these quasi-pedestrianized streets? Here are some tips:

- Search out residential areas where you see single-family dwellings
- Avoid the wide avenues, they're boring, and similar to what you'll find in any other city in the world
- Get away from billboards and neon signs
- Go against the flow of pedestrians
- When you have to choose which way to go, pick the narrowest street you can
- Be guided by green space, trees and houses with gardens
- Start walking at a small railway station —the quieter the station, the easier it will be for you to escape the crowds
- Try to choose neighborhoods that are outside the loop of the Yamanote train line

Drink vending machines can be found on every street corner in Japan.

Konbini (convenience stores) are open twenty-four hours and have food, drinks and often bathrooms.

[2] Vending Machines

The availability of drink vending machines in every part of Tokyo is a comfort factor which, once you get used to it, is difficult to live without. You have the freedom to move around in the height of summer without the fear of finding yourself in a place with nothing to drink.

There are one or two places in Japan where drink machines are hard to find, but in general these are remote mountain locations where you need to go prepared. But there are even drink machines at the summit of Mount Fuji!

[3] Convenience Stores

Convenience stores, or *konbini* in Japanese, are a little less abundant than vending machines but can also be found on many street corners. In Tokyo, they say it's a challenge to find places that don't have a konbini within a ten-minute walk.

These stores are easy to identify and have all kinds of services. In some there are even areas where you can sit and rest. In 7-Elevens you have free Wi-Fi; in others there's no Wi-Fi but you can charge your mobile phone.

What I value most about konbini is that they are a kind of gas station for people, where you can stop at any time to refill yourself. You don't just have food and drink, you also usually have access to a bathroom, trash cans, photocopier, newspapers, toiletries of all kinds and even clothes.

More and more foreigners are choosing to settle in Japan. Many of us are in Tokyo because it's a comfortable city, a *benri* (convenient) city. The konbini is a symbol of that convenience.

[4] The Rhythm of Trains

During rush hour, trains on the Yamanote Line pass through each of its thirty stations every two minutes. By the end of the day, the Yamanote Line has carried three million people. These are just the statistics from the Yamanote Line; there are dozens of other train lines, and hundreds of stations in the Greater Tokyo area. Together, they carry tens of millions of people every day.

The trains and the subway are like the working of a great, perfectly synchronized clock which almost never goes wrong. The residents of the city are like ants which have adapted to the rhythm of this machinery.

In general the train system functions to perfection, with no delays, because if something should go wrong, it starts a chain reaction that affects many people. When a train is delayed for a few seconds, there's an announcement apologizing to passengers.

It fascinates me to see how this perfectionism with train timetables affects the rhythm of the citizens. In very few parts of the world will people say

Koban are neighborhood police stations that can be of help to the traveler.

Is there a public washroom nearby?
Toire doko desu ka. トイレどこですか。

I'm lost, help me.
Michi mayoimashita, tasukete kudasai.
道迷いました、助けて下さい。

Where's the station?
Eki doko desu ka. 駅どこですか。

I'm looking for a restaurant, are there any around here?
Resutoranto sagashite imasu. Doko no hen ni resutoranto ga arimasu ka.
レストラント探しています、どこの辺にレストラントがありますか。

Thank you very much.
Arigato gozaimasu.
ありがとうございます。

to you: "Let's meet for dinner at 18:56 at exit 5B of X Station." This obsession with organizing time to the minute extends to smartphone apps that help you to organize your travel on trains, buses and all types of public transport.

As a rule the Japanese are punctual, but I'd say in Tokyo they are even more so than elsewhere.

I love to stand at station exits to watch as huge waves of people invade the sidewalks. Sitting with a cup of coffee in the Starbucks café opposite Shibuya crossing is an ideal spot to appreciate this phenomenon. The masses move following the rhythm that is set by the arrival of a train and the changing of the traffic lights at the crossing.

[5] Koban Police Boxes

Koban are tiny police boxes, some of them with room for barely one police officer. Others are a little bigger and can house a dozen or more officers. You'll know it's a koban because you'll be able to see the officer inside through the window or the door, which is nearly always open.

Besides helping to maintain public order, another function of the koban is to help lost travelers. Outside there's a map showing the most important locations in the area and almost always there's a police officer available to help you with directions. Here are some useful phrases:

[6] Each Neighborhood Has Its Own Character

They say that a mix of ideas is one of the keys to creativity, and the more varied they are, the better.

Tokyo is a creative city where lifestyles of all types intermingle in a multicolored amalgamation. It's a melting pot of ideas, which, when they come together, give rise to new fashions which sometimes go beyond the city to invade the rest of Japan, Asia and even further afield.

Harajuku is the neighborhood of the young and fashionable. A little further north, in Shinjuku, you see older people and more expensive shopping malls. If you continue on the Yamanote Line from Shinjuku you'll find yourself in Shin-Okubo, the Korean district, where the flavor of each street is unique and different to any other part of Tokyo. Further north is Sugamo, which is known as Harajuku for grandparents, with stores specializing in wigs and walking sticks.

If you go to the Shimokitazawa district, you'll find jazz clubs and secondhand clothing stores. Koenji is full of music venues where bands play to small audiences. Many stations have stores that sell items such as key rings, T-shirts or backpacks,

In Tokyo there is nothing easier to find than streets adorned with trees and plants.

all bearing the name of the neighborhood, which people buy as souvenirs.

For me it's essential to live in a creative place, and Tokyo more than fulfils the requirement. Each neighborhood is a microcosm with its own style.

[7] Trees and Plants Everywhere

There are cities such as Osaka where it's difficult to escape the concrete and the asphalt. But in Tokyo there is nothing easier to find than streets adorned with trees and plants.

Tokyo's parks are impressive, but what I enjoy most is that everywhere, when I least expect it, I come across a little green space or simply several trees which seem to defy the asphalt.

Although concrete calls the tune, I get the feeling that both residents and authorities fight back with these little details, allowing green to reconquer the city.

It's difficult to explain this phenomenon, but the photos on this page show you what I mean.

[8] Potted Plants

In areas around stations everything is invariably covered in asphalt. But once you get a little further away, you imme-

diately come across buildings surrounded by potted plants.

In other big cities, the usual thing would be to have your flowerpots on your balcony or within the privacy of your own enclosed garden, but here it doesn't seem to matter if you put your potted plants outside, right in the street.

One of the reasons you can do this is the lack of crime: you don't have to worry about anybody stealing your plants or kicking them to pieces.

Where does this mentality come from, to have plant pots outside your property? It's another manifestation of the Japanese tendency to act collectively. For example, cleaning and sweeping the sidewalk in front of your house or around each building is the responsibility of tenants — the public street sweeper is a role that doesn't exist here. This way of thinking applies also to plant pots; the community wants to have green streets, therefore each individual is responsible for looking after the pots closest to his or her house.

[9] Peace and Quiet versus Hustle and Bustle

This is a characteristic which I think is essential in any city that wants to be kind to its people. A city needs lively, bustling places, people, noise, but also

Potted plants are a common sight outside neighborhood buildings.

peaceful areas where silence can overpower the hum of traffic.

Some cities are all action and it's hard to find calm; others are boring and living in them is not very different to living in a village. Tokyo is a city that offers the two extremes. Tranquility and activity are both at your disposal. Shinjuku, through which five million commuters pass every day, is the neighborhood that never sleeps; it's somewhere you can go at three o'clock in the morning any day of the week and you'll find someone ready to party with you. But if you get tired of people, you have the option of escaping to Shinjuku Gyoen, a park not far from Shinjuku Station. There you'll find stillness, and you'll be surrounded by woods and gardens.

[10] Bicycles and Mamachari

Generally speaking, in Japan and other Asian countries, the bicycle is used to get around more than in the West, especially for short trips to places like the neighborhood supermarket.

Mamachari are a type of bicycle with a basket attached to the handlebars. Westerners might consider them unfashionable but In Japan they continue to be very popular.

Contrary to what you might think, there are very few cycle lanes in Tokyo. People cycle on the sidewalks and there are certain unwritten rules

ABOVE *Mamachari* are one of the most characteristic symbols of residential neighborhoods of Japanese cities.
BELOW Believe it or not, this picture was taken in the center of Tokyo!

[12] Creative Cafés

In general, the people of Tokyo go to cafés to have their own space outside the home to work, study, read or just lose themselves in their smartphone screens. In almost all cafés silence reigns, broken only by the sound of computer keyboards and the voices of wait staff welcoming customers.

More than 50 percent of Tokyo dwellers live alone and there are more and more people working freelance. Having a decent-sized desk and a good chair to sit in while working at the computer is a luxury in this city. It's easy and affordable to find these luxuries at the nearest café.

[13] People Almost Never Collide on Shibuya Crossing

More than half a million people use Shibuya crossing every day. It is fascinating to stop and watch the masses in motion, like flocks of migrating birds.

Just as with birds, there's an unwritten language in the movements of Tokyo pedestrians that helps the crowds to flow without colliding. Some-

that are perhaps a little bothersome for the pedestrian: for example, when you see that a bicycle is going to overtake you on the sidewalk, move to one side and don't make any sudden movements.

The bicycle is the preferred means of transport in cities and villages in Japan.

[11] Parks and Green Spaces

Tokyo is full of gigantic green lungs. In the center of the city is the Imperial Palace, which is mostly a large green space. To the west, Yoyogi Park and Meiji Jingu shrine also cover about 300 acres (120 hectares) of wooded land, helping you forget you're right next to Shibuya and Shinjuku.

Another big park is Shinjuku Gyoen. In spring it's one of the best cherry blossom viewing spots.

Other beautiful parks in Tokyo are Hamarikyu, Rikugi-en, Kitanomaru, Arisugawa-no-miya, Hibiya, Kiyosumi Garden and Kiba Park.

times, as a foreigner unaccustomed to the "subconscious," programmed movements of Tokyo pedestrians, I find it difficult not to bump into people. The trick I use is to stand behind someone and follow their footsteps. Orderly lines of people form themselves spontaneously and the most important thing is not to go against the flow. In the crowded shopping street of Takeshita-dori in Harajuku, follow one of the lines of people; if not, it's difficult to enjoy the walk.

[14] A Multi-level City

In shopping districts, building facades are covered with signs and advertisements. They indicate the types of business there are on each of the floors of the buildings.

A typical example from a neighborhood like Shinbashi might be a *monjayaki* traditional pancake restaurant on the sixth floor; a massage business on the fifth floor; on the fourth, a hairdresser; on the third, a real estate agency; on the second, a secondhand bookshop and, lastly, at street level there's a ramen restaurant.

If you don't look up, you'll miss a big part of the city.

[15] I Don't Need a Car

One of the wonders of living in Tokyo is that you don't need a car; it's a city with one of the best public transport systems in the world. You can get practically anywhere by train, and there are also multiple city bus lines to complete the network.

In other Japanese cities it's faster to move around by car, something that isn't true for Tokyo. On the occasions when a friend has gone from A to B by car within the Tokyo urban area, those of us who traveled by train almost always arrived first.

For short distances its best to cycle. It's how I moved around the neighborhoods of Shinjuku and Shibuya for ten years, although cycling on the sidewalks can be dangerous, which is why I don't do it so much any more.

RIGHT **The rainy season changes the rhythm of the city.**
FAR RIGHT **The gardens of Meiji Jingu shrine after a snowfall.**

[16] Thousands of Restaurants

According to the Statistics Bureau of Japan, there are more restaurants in the Tokyo urban area than in the whole of Europe. The range is enormous, and it's customary to eat out at lunchtime.

The great thing is that lunch menus are often very cheap. For the evening meal, depending where you go, prices can be higher.

In 2016 Tokyo was the city with the most Michelin stars in the world, followed by Kyoto and then Paris.

[17] The Rain

In Tokyo it rains a lot; sometimes it's a summer shower, other times it's week after week of continuous drizzle, with clouds covering the city in a blanket of grey.

The rain alters the color and the smells of the city, but what is most noticeable when the water hits the asphalt is the change in the mood of the people. The synchronicity normally dictated by the trains is broken, people walk more quickly and even run, others shelter in cafés or restaurants until the rain passes.

Umbrellas tinged with drops of neon color invade the streets, and you know you're in Tokyo because most of the umbrellas are transparent.

When it rains, Tokyo breathes more deeply, as if

it was concentrating before undertaking an important task, or even meditating. Some people are inconvenienced by the rain; I'm filled with an energy which inspires me to go out and take photos.

The rainy season, from the middle of June to the middle of July, is ideal if you want to see Tokyo in the rain. It's one of my favorite times to go out walking and taking photos. If you can cope with awkwardness of carrying a camera and umbrella at the same time, the constant curtain of rain gives a special flavor to everything as the metropolis moves to a different rhythm.

[18] The Snow

In Tokyo it's not as common as rain, but we usually have one or two snowfalls a year. A heavy snowfall is a the perfect opportunity to see the city in a different disguise.

No matter how long you've lived here nor how many times you've visited, if you get the chance to see Tokyo in the snow, it's something you'll never forget. Especially if you visit a temple or shrine in the early morning.

[19] Constant Change

In my second job I was able to walk to the office. I spent years passing through the same neighborhoods day after day, and I eventually realized how

> **Tips for traveling photographers**
> If you happen to be in Tokyo when a typhoon hits, get out there with your camera as soon as it passes. As the sky clears, the light is incredible and with luck you'll get photos of sunsets that suffuse the city with brilliant colors.

often houses and buildings were demolished and rebuilt, compared to what I was used to seeing in Spain. There seems to be an obsession in Tokyo with doing away with the old and building something new.

If you don't visit a Tokyo neighborhood for a few years, you're likely to find it has changed significantly when you return. The average lifespan of a building in Tokyo is barely forty years or even less in certain central areas.

For example, if you walked around Shibuya in 2015 and you go back now, you'd find it unrecognizable! The good news is that the Hachiko dog statue is still in the same place in front of the station.

If we analyze this through the Prism of Natural Disasters, the "logical" thing is to think that since nothing is going to last, it's better to keep on renewing everything before it's destroyed. Also, the government is continually forcing the renewal process by changing the standards to which buildings must comply in order to withstand earthquakes. In 1981 the regulations were made tougher and it's more and more difficult to find pre-1981 buildings in Tokyo.

I used to be overcome by a mixture of sadness and nostalgia on seeing streets I'd known for years disappearing and being transformed into something new. Now I allow myself to be surprised by this city which, like the phoenix, is constantly being reborn.

[20] Infinity and Fractality

If ever I'm traveling out of Tokyo with visitors from overseas, they might ask me after half an hour "Where are we?" and I'll answer "In Tokyo." An hour later we have the same conversation: "Where are we?," "In Tokyo . . ."

Tokyo seems to go on forever and beyond. The Greater Tokyo area in its entirety occupies every corner of the Kanto Plain, stretching more than sixty miles (one hundred kilometers) in length and another sixty miles in width.

The strange thing is that all the neighborhoods share a certain DNA, with particular elements that constantly repeat themselves on different scales, like a never-ending fractal.

When I get off the train in a Tokyo neighborhood that I'm sure I've never visited before, I can't avoid the feeling that its streets seem familiar to me and that perhaps I've already been there. As you get to know Tokyo, you experience a constant sensation of déjà vu.

[21] The Feeling of Freedom

Tokyo is a city of possibilities. On the weekend you can book a place at a seminar on bonsai care with

The mass of buildings and houses stretches as far as the eye can see, from the sea to the mountains, occupying the whole of the Kanto Plain.

one of the world's greatest experts, or if you prefer, go to a concert by a world-famous band who are on the Japan leg of their tour.

You have at your disposal art exhibitions brought from the world's greatest collections to Tokyo galleries; you can study at dozens of universities (the city is home to more than ten winners of the Nobel Prize); the neighborhood of Shibuya is full of technology multinationals where you can work and earn a living if you choose to; and the district of Marunouchi is full of finance companies.

If you like to have a good time, there's Roppongi, which after dark has some of the best nightlife in Asia. Even Hollywood actors fly out to Tokyo to party in Roppongi.

Thanks to the bullet train, if you set out early in the morning, you can spend the day skiing in the mountains in winter, or surfing in the sea in summer and come back home to Tokyo in the evening.

If you like peace and quiet, you have at your disposal bookshops, public libraries in every

LEFT, TOP and CENTER I could have chosen to become a Godzilla maker.
BOTTOM People enjoy the sunset at Yoyogi Park, one the places in Tokyo where you can escape from the concrete sprawl. Visit at the weekend to see gatherings of various fashion "tribes."

neighborhood, museums, art galleries, gardens and parks, cafés . . .

The possibilities are so numerous that the problem is choosing what to do. Which hobby do I choose? What shall I do at the weekend? Where shall I work?

Once I was lucky enough to meet one of Japan's greatest experts in building Godzilla figures. He was so friendly that he tried to persuade me to come to his studio and he'd teach me how to make a Godzilla. He was so passionate about what he did, he almost convinced me.

Here's a list of some of the things you can do in Tokyo: tortilla-making, flamenco dancing, grow wasabi mustard, learn how to use a katana sword, or two at the same time, learn how to serve sushi on a naked body (*nyotaimori*), practice archery on horseback, learn how to cook *chahan* fried rice, or attend exercise classes that will help you sculpt the sexiest ass possible . . .

Having so many possibilities makes for an addictive sense of freedom, but very often you just feel overwhelmed and end up staying at home in classic *hikikomori* recluse style.

[22] Nobody Judges You

One of the first things I notice when I leave Japan is that strangers tend to look at me much more.

Why does nobody look at you in the street here?

In general terms, the Japanese tend to follow the dictates of *wa* (和: peace, absence of conflict): maintaining peace and avoiding conflict. To look directly at a stranger is considered as an intrusion into the other person's privacy. Meeting someone's eye can cause tension and is something to be avoided at all costs.

You inevitably feel a sense of lightness when you walk the streets of Tokyo. Nobody looks at you any more or less no matter what you're wearing, or however extravagant your hairstyle. Thanks to this, the streets of Tokyo are a kind of laboratory from which all kinds of fashion emerge.

This sense of anonymity – that nobody's watching you, that you can dress and follow any fashion without being judged by anyone – is liberating.

[23] Safety

Japan is safe, which makes certain aspects of life here free from anxiety and very convenient.

It's quite normal to see schoolchildren as young as six going to school alone on the subway. You also often see children playing in the street, making the most of outdoor spaces.

Other signs that demonstrate the safety of Japan include seeing people asleep everywhere, being able to leave your things on the table in a café and go to the bathroom without worrying, or not having to put several high-security locks on your bicycle to stop it from being stolen.

[24] Pedestrians Have Right of Way

People who've spent some time traveling in Japan have on occasion told me that right of way for pedestrians at crosswalks isn't observed. And he or she wouldn't be wrong: if there's a crosswalk, or there are no stop lights, never trust cars. For some reason that I haven't yet managed to work out, in these particular cases vehicles almost always ignore pedestrians, and crossing the road can be dangerous. Yes, cars do jump the crosswalks, so watch out!

But, as though to compensate for this, there are certain areas of the city where the number of pedestrians is much higher than the number of vehicles, which have no choice but to get swallowed up by the huge crowds of passersby. This tends to happen in shopping districts, especially at week-ends, and also in narrow streets. In these places, the pedestrian is king.

[25] Shopping Streets

Shotengai 商店街 are streets or groups of several streets, close to a railway station, that are home to shops of all types. Shotengai are usually pedestrianized, and if they're not, most cars don't dare drive down them. Some shotengai are covered, which make them an ideal place to spend time on rainy days.

There's something of a village atmosphere in a shotengai; you get the feeling that people have known each other for years. Customers talk to shopkeepers about the weather or neighborhood politics, you see people stopping to say hello to acquaintances or children running around with their friends.

[26] Yellow Tiles on the Sidewalks

The main purpose of yellow tiles marked with circular studs is to guide visually-impaired people around the streets of Tokyo. But they also help other travelers; for example they are used to

BELOW **The pedestrian is king in Tokyo's shopping streets.**
FACING PAGE, LEFT **Yellow tiles on the sidewalks.**
FACING PAGE, RIGHT **See-through umbrellas have a special appeal that's almost photogenic.**

indicate how close to the edge you can stand on station platforms.

Aesthetically, yellow is garish and can seem to spoil the sidewalk, but you grow attached to it. Yellow lines are one of the almost unmistakable signs that you are in a Japanese street.

[27] Retro Style

The Showa 昭和 era began in 1926 and ended in 1989. Then from 1989 to 2019 came the Heisei 平成 era. Now we are in the Reiwa 令和 era.

The oldest neighborhoods or districts of Tokyo still have buildings and restaurants whose appearance hasn't changed since the Showa era; they are said to be *Showa-fu* 昭和風 (in the Showa style). Walking around these retro places is like a journey into the Tokyo of the past.

[28] See-through Umbrellas

See-through umbrellas have a been a feature of Japan for decades, and inspired Ridley Scott when he was staging one of the early scenes of the 1982 movie *Blade Runner*.

Why are there so many see-through umbrellas? I don't know, but they look great, you can see where you're going easily, and they're so cheap that if you lose them it doesn't matter. "See-through" is to umbrellas what Bic is to ballpoint pens.

All *konbini* convenience stores sell cheap see-though umbrellas. They're so abundant that if

you go into a store and leave yours in the umbrella stand, you're unlikely to find it when you come out of the store. If you put an identifying mark on it, you'll avoid confusion and you'll also help others to avoid taking your umbrella by mistake.

[29] Spotless Trains

After home, office (or café in the case of freelancers), we residents of Tokyo spend most of our time inside trains. The Japanese consider the train as an extension their home, and they act accordingly. Trains are always spotless. Seats are soft and comfortable. You can spend hours on a train reading manga, playing video games or even working. In summer trains are air-conditioned, and you can choose between warmer and colder cars. In winter there is heating under the seats. Train travel can be so pleasant that sometimes you don't want your stop to arrive. Some train lines have special cars only for women during peak rush-hour periods.

Of course there are also the famous trains crammed with passengers, when you can't wait to get off. But if you avoid the rush hour you'll almost always find a place to sit. If you don't want to travel in packed trains, avoid using them between seven thirty and nine thirty in the morning and five and seven in the evening.

[31] Museums

If you like escaping into other worlds, whether real or imaginary, the range of museums and exhibitions in Tokyo is practically unlimited. There are more than a thousand museums and art galleries in the city. In the Ueno Park area alone there are eight museums. Some of them are worth visiting just for the beauty of the buildings themselves. The National Art Center in Roppongi and the Edo-Tokyo Museum in Ryogoku are housed in impressive buildings.

If you can, avoid the weekends so you don't have to queue. The website tokyoartbeat.com lists galleries and museums in each area, along with current exhibitions and opening hours.

[32] Cleanliness

Another thing that still surprises me about Japan is coming across the person in charge of a building cleaning the sidewalk around it with care and diligence. But when I look closely it turns out that the sidewalk is already clean; it doesn't need cleaning because not enough time has elapsed since the last time it was cleaned. Even so, the person persists in cleaning it and will come back to carry out the same job the following day at the same time.

Cleaning what it is already clean would seem absurd to us, but here the important thing is the

The Best Sunset Views in Tokyo

Bunkyo-ku Civic Center
Two minutes' walk from Suidobashi Station (it's signposted as you leave the station). The twenty-fifth floor is open to the public and entry is free.

Tokyo Metropolitan Government Building, Shinjuku
Ten minutes from the station. Entrance to the observation decks is free.

Tokyo City View and Sky Deck, Roppongi Hills
Entry costs a thousand yen. There is also a museum on the lower floors for which you need to pay an extra fee.

[30] Sunset Views

Tokyo extends across a huge area, but it doesn't have one single city center with impossibly tall skyscrapers like New York or Shanghai. Tokyo has several centers each of which has clusters of tall buildings. Though the skyline is not as spectacular as elsewhere, the low concentration of skyscrapers allows you to enjoy beautiful views from even the tenth floor of a building in almost any location in the city. When the sun is setting look for a tall building and head up to the rooftop; if you're lucky you'll see Mount Fuji on the horizon watching over the metropolis. The elusive mountain isn't always easy to see, but you have a better chance on a clear winter day or when the sky clear after a typhoon or a heavy rainstorm.

process; the act of cleaning is more important than the usefulness of the work. This mentality transfers to many other aspects of Japanese life: the important thing is to do something well and in a methodical way, over and over again.

Some areas are so clean that when you find yourself someplace that's dirtier and more chaotic than usual it really stands out. If you go into the alleyways of the entertainment districts of Kabukicho, Dogenzaka or Roppongi, you'll come across the authentic smell of the Tokyo sewers, with trash blowing about everywhere and the occasional rat out for a stroll. But these are exceptions; Tokyo is generally clean.

[33] Power Lines

One way to check if a photo was taken in Japan — as opposed to another Asian country with similar scenery — is to look for utility poles and cables, which are omnipresent in almost every urban area.

"So advanced in some ways but their streets are full of cables?" said Mr. Casca as he walked with Ms. Wonder through the streets of Kyoto.

"You ought to be more understanding," she replied.

"Understanding? They could put them underground. They make everything look ugly," answered Mr. Casca.

"Look at it through the Prism of Natural Disasters you learned about in the book I gave you," explained Ms. Wonder. "It's safer to have the cables above ground in an earthquake zone."

As Ms. Wonder said, having electrical cables overground is less risky in a country where earthquakes are frequent. It depends on the terrain, but in general if they're buried they cost more to repair, whereas if they're above ground they still break but they're easier to fix. After a powerful earthquake I've watched as trucks full of workers immediately go round checking the cables in the streets.

But Mr. Casca was right about one thing: they do look ugly. Cables ruin your travel photos. The best thing to do is to edit them out, unless you want to make the cables the subject of your photo.

If Mount Fuji appears before you at sunset and a couple of cables are ruining your photo you'll have to move around until you find an angle where no cables are visible. This is a "trick" that everyone uses. Sometimes you see beautiful photos on the Internet or in travel guides, but when you see the scene in real life you're slightly disappointed to see cables everywhere except in the exact spot where the photo was taken.

Although cables are ugly, you do grow fond of them. What would the streets of Japan be without them? It's a brand that's 100 per cent Japanese. In some parts of Tokyo they're starting to bury cabling and when this happens the city seems to be losing an important part of its identity.

[34] Pay Phones

Although the number of smartphones is greater than the number of inhabitants, you can still find public pay phones in Tokyo. Fewer and fewer people use them, but even so they're still an integral part

of the urban landscape. I love their retro-futuristic look and the nostalgia they induce.

[35] Cats

They are abundant in the novels of Haruki Murakami, and also in the streets of Tokyo. Coming across cats is a sign that you're in a quiet neighborhood.

[36] Hidden Temples and Shrines

It's always a pleasant surprise to find a small Shinto shrine tucked away among other buildings.

Sometimes we assume that a sacred place must be grand and formal, but it doesn't have to be. A tiny temples or shrine squeezed between two little houses is something that often grabs the attention of Westerners traveling in Asian countries.

In the case of Shinto, sometimes all that's needed to be considered a shrine is a little *torii* gate peeping out of a gap between buildings.

[37] Five O'clock Music

In almost every corner of the city, especially near schools, parks and official institutions, powerful loudspeakers are installed that play a tune every afternoon at five o'clock. The loudspeakers are there in case of disaster, to provide alarm signals and information to the population. The music you hear every day at five is a test of the loudspeaker system.

But the music has other uses. Many people

ABOVE **Finding friendly cats in the streets of Tokyo is really cool.**
ABOVE RIGHT **In Tokyo you can still find lots of telephone booths and landline phones operated with coins or cards.**

BELOW The population of crows in Japan is enormous.
RIGHT Harajuku is one of the best places in Tokyo to stroll
around and look at what people are wearing.

believe that the five o'clock music is the signal for kids to go home. Although this is not its primary purpose, I like this belief because it's more romantic than the true reason for the music. I ought not to feel nostalgic for my own childhood because as I child I didn't live here, but I can't help but feel a pang of melancholy every time I hear the five o'clock melody.

The music is also useful for adults as a reminder to drive more carefully through neighborhoods where children are heading for home.

The tune that is played differs from neighborhood to neighborhood, but one of the most commonly used – especially in Tokyo – is *Yukake Koyake* 夕焼け小焼け (夕 sunset; 焼け burn; 小 little; 焼け burn). It was composed by a schoolteacher called Uko Nakamura eighty years ago. In the city of Hachioji, where the writer of the song was born, there's a bus stop called Yukake Koyake. Here is a translation of the song's lyrics:

> *The sunset tinged with red*
> *marks the irretrievable passing of time.*
> *When we hear the ringing of the bell of the*
> *mountain temple,*
> *with the crows, let us go home, hand in hand.*
> *When we get home*
> *the big round moon rises.*
> *When the little birds are dreaming,*
> *the golden glow of the stars fills the night sky.*

[38] Street Fashion

Some of the most interesting places for people watching are the streets of Shibuya, particularly the youth mecca of Harajuku.

Shibuya is the heart of Japan as far as fashion is concerned. In the side streets of Harajuku, tiny shops come and go all the time; those that fail disappear to make room for other labels. Those that make it expand their business, opening new, bigger franchises throughout Shibuya, perhaps in the

famous 109 shopping mall. If they continue to be successful they spread across Asia and sometimes the world.

If you're a creative person, or just curious, Shibuya is the perfect place to collect ideas as you walk around.

[39] Cawing Crows

One of the earliest memories I have of Japan is waking up on my first morning in a six-tatami-mat room in the Suginami neighborhood of Tokyo to a mysterious noise coming from outside. I opened the curtains to find out what the racket could be, and discovered a flock of cawing crows circling the garden and perching in the trees.

ABOVE Elevated freeways are one of the features of the Tokyo landscape.
RIGHT A stroll down a Japanese street can reveal a whole universe of small details.

[40] Elevated Expressways

Whereas in the West we tend to build tunnels for road traffic, here the traditional thing is to elevate the freeways. In Osaka there's a section of elevated freeway that goes through a building, and here in Tokyo there are areas where as many as three levels of freeway are stacked up, reaching heights equivalent to an eight- or nine-story building.

It's fascinating to walk underneath these freeways, especially at night, and to feel as though you're in a city straight out of a cyberpunk movie. It's also great to drive along them at night, feeling as though you're flying and with a whole new perspective on the city.

[41] Little Details

I'm always amazed when I walk down a street for the umpteenth time and I see a particular detail I'd never noticed before. It could be a decoration hanging from the roof of a restaurant, ornaments hidden in a plant pot, drawings or art on a wall ... If you walk slowly and pay attention you'll discover a whole universe of little things that make strolling through Tokyo an adventure every time.

[42] Bus Stops

In the more populated areas, bus stops have a roof and a bench to sit on, but in neighborhoods further away from the city center most of the bus stops are simply a post, with a timetable attached. In many cases, to compensate for the lack of bench, you'll find a row of old, mismatched chairs next to the post, donated by the residents of the neighborhood.

[43] Nightlife

In most Tokyo neighborhoods there is no nightlife. At night it's a quiet city.

If you're looking for bars, restaurants or nightclubs there are only certain neighborhoods where you can find a party atmosphere until the early hours on any day of the week: Roppongi, Shibuya, Shinjuku and certain parts of Ginza, Shinbashi and Marunouchi.

[44] Microbars

Tiny bars and restaurants with room for ten diners or fewer are one of the more exotic characteristics of Tokyo and of other Japanese cities, too. I still

remember clearly a scene from the 1982 movie *Blade Runner* in which Harrison Ford enjoys a bowl of ramen at the narrow counter of a restaurant that doesn't even have walls.

The most famous microbar districts of Tokyo are Nombei Yokocho, next to Shibuya Station; Golden Gai in Shinjuku (very touristy these days), and under the train tracks between Yurakucho and Shinbashi stations.

[45] Stop Signs on the Streets

Tomare 止まれ means "stop" in Japanese. Besides appearing on road signs, it's also written vertically on the asphalt at many junctions. Seeing the three characters at my feet when I'm walking along fills

me with a strong sense of place and also with nostalgia, perhaps because it was one of the first Japanese words I learned how to read.

[46] No Trash Cans

"Such a drag that you can't find a trash can! I've been walking around with this piece of trash in my pocket for two hours and I can't find anywhere to put it." These are the most typical complaints you hear from people traveling around Japan for the first time.

But it's not the city that is obliged to provide a trash can on every corner, it's the traveler who has to adapt and find a way to get rid of his or her trash. This change of mentality passes responsibility from the city to the citizen, and as a result, contrary to what you might think, the streets — generally speaking — are cleaner.

In fact, the underlying reason for the disappearance of trash cans in public places in Japan is the 1995 sarin gas attack on the Tokyo subway, which was carried out using gas canisters hidden in trash cans.

You can actually find trash cans, but not in the places Westerners might be accustomed to. In the case of subway stations, the trash cans are found

ABOVE Tiny lanes packed with traditional bars have a retro-futuristic feel.
RIGHT The word 止まれ is written vertically on the asphalt so it's easy to read as you approach in your car.

just as you go through the turnstiles. If you're not used to them, from a distance they don't look like trash cans; they have a small opening and a transparent panel at the front.

Another place to throw away trash is in *konbini* convenience stores. Sometimes konbini will have trash cans outside, but more commonly you'll find them inside the shop.

Bottles and cans are easier to dispose of because next to any vending machine there's usually a trash can where you can put them. Once you open your eyes and start looking more closely you'll see that trash cans are everywhere.

[47] Shibuya Crossing
If Tokyo is the heart of Japan, Shibuya is the heart of Tokyo, and Shibuya Crossing is the heart of Shibuya. In fact, the famous street crossing is really the pulse of the neighborhood, with hun-

If Tokyo is the heart of Japan, Shibuya is the heart of Tokyo, and Shibuya Crossing is the heart of Shibuya.

dreds of thousands of people surging from one side to the other every day in continuous waves of human energy.

Shibuya is one of those places that's difficult to explain to people who haven't been there. No matter how many photos or videos of the place you see, nothing compares to the experience of standing next to the Hachiko dog statue outside the station, a popular meeting point. Nor can you explain how it truly feels to navigate the vast crossing beneath gigantic advertising screens, trying to find a path through the crowds, until after a while you realize that you're just another person following the invisible lines created by a shared "Shibuyan understanding" generated by the mass of humanity of which you are a part.

[48] Old Houses
The streets of Tokyo are dotted with old houses. Some have aged well, others badly. I like finding old places because they open a doorway into the past of the city.

LEFT Tokyo is full of unexpected tranquil corners, even in the busiest and most commercial of neighborhoods.
BELOW It is said that the 1982 movie *Blade Runner* as well as the novels of William Gibson were inspired by the aesthetic of the streets and neighborhoods of Tokyo.

[49] Relaxing Spots

Tokyo and other Japanese cities are somehow able to create little nooks to relax in, despite the abundance of concrete. When you least expect it, even in the busiest and most commercial of neighborhoods, you're bound to stumble across a tranquil corner in a little side street.

[50] Cyberpunk Tokyo

Cyberpunk is a science-fiction genre that emerged in the 1980s. The novels of William Gibson and the 1982 movie *Blade Runner* are considered pioneers of the cyberpunk style. It's said that both William Gibson and Ridley Scott (the director of *Blade Runner*) were inspired by the aesthetic of the streets and neighborhoods of Osaka and Tokyo, lit up by neon after nightfall.

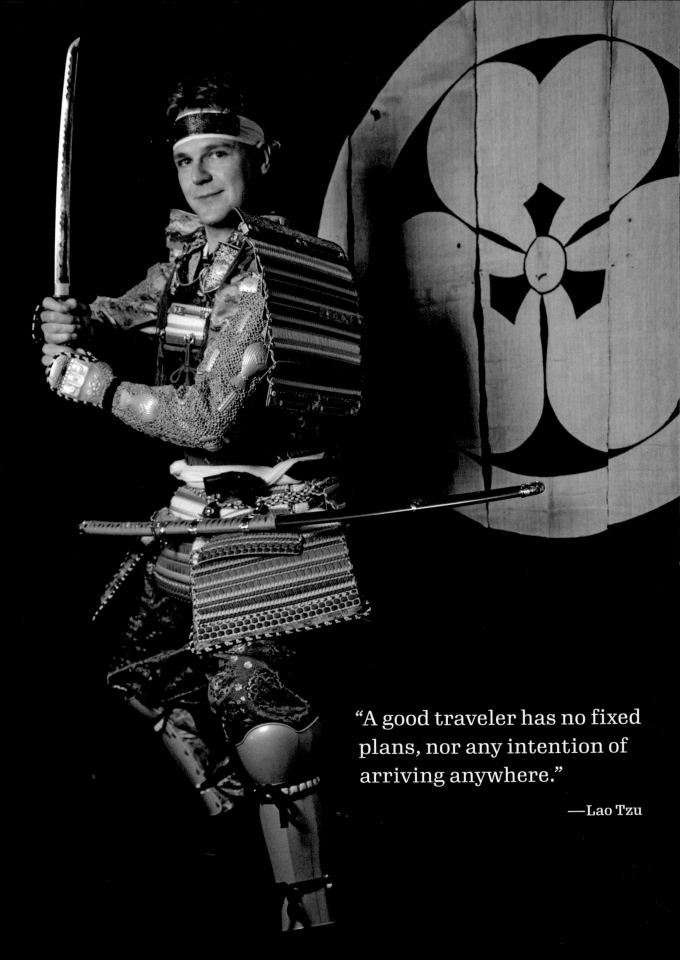

"A good traveler has no fixed plans, nor any intention of arriving anywhere."

—Lao Tzu

CHAPTER 9
My Japan Travel Diaries

After arriving in Tokyo and settling into life in the city, my first explorations of the country took in the most famous destinations: Nikko, Kamakura, Kyoto, Nara, Osaka, Kobe and Hiroshima. In my first book, A Geek in Japan, *I introduce the places I consider unmissable.*

I've made several journeys to those essential destinations and I always recommend them to people traveling around Japan for the first time. But if you want to visit places that are a little different to the conventional ones, over time I've discovered other lesser-known gems, which I'm going to talk about in this chapter.

Lately, to choose destinations that are more "adventurous" than usual, I look at a map of Japan and I pick at random a prefecture I've never visited. (Japan is divided into forty-seven prefectures, including Tokyo and Osaka, both of which have the distinction of being both prefecture and city. They are kind of city-states, even having laws that are different to those of other prefectures.)

Most of the population of Japan lives in the prefectures of Tokyo, Kanagawa, Saitama, Chiba, Osaka and Aichi. The first four of those prefectures are concentrated on the Kanto Plain, forming one of the most densely

LEFT **The author dressed as a samurai.**
RIGHT **A traveler waits at a sleepy rural station.**

populated urban areas in the world with forty million inhabitants.

In this chapter I will describe some of my travels around Japan. My goal is not to provide a travel guide, but simply to inspire you.

To organize your own travel, I think the best tool you can use these days is the Internet, where you can always find up to date train and transport timetables and maps. Recently there is more and more information in English about Japanese destinations.

Everything changes so fast in Japan that printed information becomes obsolete very quickly. My advice is always to confirm via the Internet or by telephone any travel-related information you find in this book, or any other.

"Each region and prefecture of Japan has its own personality."

10 Tips for Travelers

[1] Don't Worry

This is my number one piece of advice to all those traveling in Japan for the first time.

Japan is one of the safest places in the world, which gives you the freedom to explore without fear. Don't be scared of getting lost, because if the worst comes to the worst all you have to do is ask someone how to get to the nearest train station.

It can seem intimidating to go half way round the world and touch down in this place full of strange writing that we can't decipher. But to tell the truth, once you get used to using the trains and realize how safe it is, you immediately gain confidence and it becomes easy and even enjoyable to travel around.

The less afraid you become and the less you worry, the more adventures you'll have.

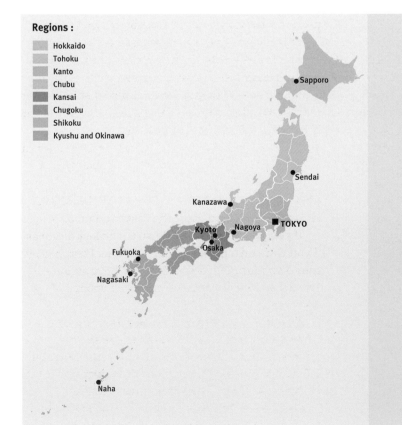

Regions :

- Hokkaido
- Tohoku
- Kanto
- Chubu
- **Kansai**
- Chugoku
- Shikoku
- Kyushu and Okinawa

県 Prefectures

The suffix –ken 県 in Japanese means prefecture. For example, if we're talking about Aomori (青森) to refer to the prefecture rather than the city, we would say Aomori-ken (青森県). For Nagano Prefecture (長野), it would be Nagano-ken (長野県) and so on for all the other prefectures.

The exceptions are Osaka and Tokyo. Although they are considered prefectures, they don't use the suffix –ken, but the suffixes –fu 府 and –to 都 respectively, making them Osaka-fu 大阪府 and Tokyo-to 東京都.

Japan's forty-seven prefectures are grouped into eight geographical regions as shown on the map.

Trying restaurants which catch your attention as you're walking down the street can add serendipity to your journey.

[2] Walk Everywhere

Walking is one of the best ways to get to know a new place. If it's a village, lose yourself in its lanes; if it's a big city, choose a neighborhood and wander around its streets.

If you want to discover the livelier areas, watch the flow of people along the streets and follow it. Normally this will lead you to the busier districts. In Japanese cities, another of the subliminal signs you can follow is the neon. The more lights and adverts you can see, the more likely it is that you're close to a big station.

If you want the opposite, if you like peace and quiet and you're curious to find homely neighborhoods like the ones you've seen in *Doraemon* or *Shinchan* anime shows, walk away from the neon signs and you'll soon find residential areas. Though less spectacular, they're also fascinating places to explore and ones you'd probably never see if you were following a guide book.

I've been walking around Tokyo for fifteen years and I feel there's still a lot left to discover.

[3] Leave Time for Improvisation

Plan the basics and leave the rest to chance.

If you plan everything down to the last detail as if you were on a package tour, you'll feel trapped by your own plan. The best thing is to have an appropriate balance between planned and spontaneous activities.

I'll admit that as far as some things are concerned, it's difficult not to plan in Japan, and there's not much you can do about that. In chapter 6, for example, I explained that if you want to go the Ghibli Museum you'll have to buy your ticket beforehand. If you want to stay in a good hotel in the center of Tokyo or in a good ryokan in a popular

---

MY TRAVEL TIPS
Best Apps for Planning Journeys Around Japan

In addition to Google Maps, there are other great travel apps that you can get from your smartphone's app store.

Tokyo Subway Navigation A fantastic Tokyo subway app. It's impossible to get lost if you're using this.

Japan Travel This has maps and train routes for the whole of Japan. It can help you decide whether or not to invest in a Japan Rail Pass, and it also recommends places to visit in each location.

Hyperpedia More trains and travel routes.

Gurunavi An app for finding and booking restaurants, with useful restaurant ratings.

Tokyoartbeat Museums, exhibitions and arts events.

A traditional Japanese *sento* bath house exhibit at the Edo-Tokyo Open Air Architectural Museum.

One day, when we went walking in the Okutama Mountains on the outskirts of Tokyo, we met a Japanese man who'd spent years traveling around South America and who spoke Spanish. Halfway through the walk he introduced us to some friends of his who lived in the area. They invited us to eat and drink with them in a house surrounded by the greenery of the forest. Later they showed us how to dig for wild *takenoko* (bamboo shoots), which we took home to cook the next day.

[5] Spend Time in One Place

If it's your first visit to Japan and you have limited time, don't try to tour the entire country. For example, a basic mistake is having a plan that tries to take in Tokyo, Nikko, Hakone, Kanazawa, Kyoto, Osaka, Kobe, Hiroshima, and Nagasaki. If your schedule is too crammed you won't have time to enjoy each place.

Don't lurch from one side of the country to the other on the bullet train. You'll spend your whole trip inside trains. It's better to see fewer places in less of a hurry.

Traveling isn't a competition to see how many names of cities you can tick off in your travel diary; the aim is to savor and enjoy a culture that's not your own.

Give yourself plenty of time in each location you visit. It's on those slow days when you haven't planned much that you'll probably discover things you'd never find if you were dashing from hotel to hotel. Ten days in Kyoto? Are you afraid you'll get bored? Don't worry, even if you lived in that city for several years you'd never get to know all of it. There are more than 1,600 Buddhist temples and 400 Shinto shrines in Kyoto. It would take you more than five years to see them all!

tourist destination like Hakone, you also have to book quite a long way in advance.

In all the big cities in high season hotels are always full, so you should book your room well in advance. My advice is to book accommodation months before, at least in cities and tourist areas, unless you don't mind sleeping in capsule hotels or in *manga kissa* (manga cafés). You should also book in advance activities that you absolutely don't want to miss.

[4] Talk to the Locals

Japanese people are shy by nature but many of them want to practice their English.

If you smile and try talking in English to the people you meet, you'll find that some are able to hold a conversation and they'll give you local information which you'd never find out about on your own.

[6] Look for Activities

Rather than rushing from one place to the next, seek out activities you can get involved in. There are more and more things on offer, both online and at tourist offices.

For example you could get dressed up as a geisha or samurai, take part in a tea ceremony, meditate in a temple, take a class in a traditional art such as pottery or ikebana, or maybe a cooking class . . . the list is endless.

[7] Nightlife Areas

The best way to get to know the locals is to go into bars or nightclubs. At night in the drinking hot spots, people are much more outgoing and some of them speak better English than you might expect. With luck you'll end the night with new friends, one of whom will surely insist on being your guide and taking you somewhere interesting in the area the next day.

I hadn't planned to end up at this concert where robots played the instruments for human dancers. It was only because I said yes to a friend's invitation.

[8] Say Yes to Everything?

Saying yes to everything that's suggested to you can be a good way to discover fabulous places and to end up in interesting situations, such as at a local festival, for example. But it can also be a recipe for finishing up in awkward situations or even wasting your time in a tourist trap.

My own policy is normally to say no to everything, with the occasional yes thrown in when I'm in the mood for adventure.

The author is not responsible for what may happen if you follow a strict "yes to everything" policy for long periods of time!

[9] Add Serendipity

If we plan every last minute of our travels with no space for spontaneity we don't leave room for interesting and unexpected things to happen. Travel unhurriedly, see fewer places but give them more time. Have a plan for the start of the day but not for later on — allow serendipity to be your guide.

Don't rigorously follow what your guidebooks tell you, not even what I tell you in this book. Follow your intuition wherever it leads you and that way you'll have unique stories to take home with you.

Here are some ways you can add serendipity to your travels:

- Combine planning with randomness, for example, book a special restaurant one day, the rest of the time try restaurants that catch your attention as you're walking down the street.
- If you're tired of seeing tourist sights, move away a little from the hustle and bustle and go into a café in a quiet area. Spend a little time enjoying a cup of tea or coffee and a spot of people-watching.
- Rent a room in a shared house, make friends with your housemates and go along with their plans.
- Get off the train at a random station. If it has a tourist office ask what there is to do in the area, if not, just go for a stroll and see what you find.

[10] Start with a Photo

There are photos that capture my imagination with such intensity I can't help wanting to know more about the place where they were taken. These days, thanks to the Internet, it's easy to find the location of a photo.

Once I know the place, I plan a trip there, just to be able to contemplate the scene myself. Besides being able to see with my own eyes what I'd only seen before in the photograph and in my imagination, I can take home with me my own photo as well as the experience of another travel adventure.

Karuizawa

When I finished writing my book *Forest Bathing: The Rejuvenating Practice of Shinrin Yoku*, a little voice inside my head told me that I had to go back to Karuizawa. This small town, situated in the east of Nagano Prefecture, is a favored weekend destination for many Tokyo residents, whether in summer to escape the suffocating heat of the city, or in winter to enjoy its ski slopes. It also has the honor of being the only place in the world to have been a venue for Olympic events in both the summer games (equestrianism) — and winter (curling).

Karuizawa doesn't have a huge number of tourist attractions, but it's perfect for relaxing surrounded by nature. It's a town whose center isn't easy to find when you're walking around its streets. Houses are scattered in every direction, and their roofs are hidden by trees, mingling with the green of nature.

It's not a traditional destination for a first-time visitor to Japan, but I know people who love it because of how different it is to the rest of the country. It looks like a Swiss town that has landed in the middle of Japan.

Karuizawa was a relatively unknown village until the Canadian missionary Alexander Croft Shaw visited it in 1888. He liked it so much that he made his home there and established a small Anglican church.

Since then it's been a favorite holiday destination of many diplomats stationed in Japan. It's also the chosen place of rest and relaxation for Emperor Akihito. As a young man he liked to play tennis in Karuizawa, and it's said that it was here that he first fell in love with Michiko, who became his wife.

John Lennon and Yoko Ono also visited Karuizawa several times and always stayed in the famous Mikasa Hotel, which is now a museum.

As the area is mountainous, the best way to get around is by car. We hired one next to Karuizawa Station — where the *shinkansen* bullet train stops — and we headed off to explore the forests to the north.

A few miles into our journey, when the road began to climb steeply, we parked at the starting point of a hiking route. A blast of rejuvenating air

The Shiraito Falls (lit.,"white thread falls") in Karuizawa is one of the most visited places in the area.

Waterfall of the White Threads" 白糸の滝 (白 white; 糸 thread; の of; 滝 waterfall). In contrast to the walk we'd just done, Shiraito was full of tourists, as it's one of the most popular destinations in Karuizawa.

The waterfall is only 10 feet (3 meters) high, but 230 feet (70 meters) wide, forming a curtain of water with a unique appearance. Its name describes it well; it looks as though multiple streams of water are emerging as if by magic from the forest. The mountains here have several horizontal layers of volcanic rock which force the water out.

The water comes from the nearby Mount Asama volcano (2,548 meters in altitude, last eruption in 2009). The information panel explains that when the winter snow melts on the volcano, the water travels very slowly, for six years, until it gushes out at the waterfall.

energized us as we stepped out of the car and set off on foot through the majestic forests of the Japanese Alps. We didn't meet anyone else during our entire hike; we were accompanied only by the birds and the rustling of the wind in the trees.

I was fascinated by the range of greens to be seen, some so bright they seemed to shine. They say that May is the best month to visit Japanese forests because this is the season when each variety of tree displays its color to its maximum splendor.

We followed a stream, crossed a wooden bridge and eventually stopped to relax at Ryukaeno Falls, whose name literally means "which gives back to the dragons." A wooden panel has the name of the waterfall written in large letters: 竜返の滝 (竜 dragon: 返 give back; の of; 滝 waterfall).

Another sign warned us of the danger of bears, which are more and more numerous in the mountains of Japan. The notice explained that bears in the Japanese Alps are timid and that the best thing to do is to keep them at bay with loud conversation and avoid walking alone in silence.

On our way back to the car we came across a dead fox, a scene that could have been straight out of a zombie movie. We couldn't help wondering how the fox had died . . .

We drove a few more miles along the mountain road, which became narrower and narrower, until we reached the car park for the Shiraito Falls, "The

The Mikasa Hotel, built in 1905, is now a museum you can visit.

After a few hours enjoying the forest we went back to the town and parked our car next to the former Mikasa Hotel, which is now a museum. We bought tickets and went inside to explore this place where famous people from all over the world used to stay when they visited Japan.

It was built in 1905 and the exterior looks central European. It has two floors with spacious rooms and high, bright windows.

In the Meiji period (1868–1912) when Japan first started opening up to Western influences after centuries of isolation, many buildings were constructed in the Western style. The Mikasa Hotel is considered to be one of the finest examples in Japan of a building that imitates European architecture. It was constructed using the same materials and methods as those used in Europe at the time. Nowadays it's registered by the Japanese government as a national treasure.

A café-restaurant also serves as a reception area, where a piano that surely hasn't been touched for decades stands next to one of the fireplaces that would have heated the building in the winter. The wide staircase in the center of the hotel reminded me of a scene from a Hollywood horror movie. As we finished our tour a couple of newlyweds arrived to have some photos taken.

During our remaining days in Karuizawa we continued to explore nature, bathing in the green forests — practicing *shinrin yoku* — and taking photos of country cottages that seemed to come straight from the pages of *Heidi*.

How to Get There

Karuizawa From Tokyo Station take the Hokuriku bullet train bound for Nagano, and get off at Karuizawa Station.
Mikasa Hotel It's best to hire a car next to the station. (You'll need an international driving licence.) You can also get there by bus. Take the no. 2 bound for Kusatsu from the north exit of Karuizawa Station. It stops near the hotel.

Fukushima and Miyagi

On March 11, 2011, an earthquake of magnitude 9.1 struck the coast of northeastern Japan, followed by a tsunami. In Fukushima and Miyagi prefectures the consequences were devastating, with 15,897 people confirmed dead and another 2,533 still missing today.

I was in Tokyo when the earthquake happened, and thankfully the city wasn't badly affected. But I still recall with dread the moment when I watched from my desk as buildings across the city, including my own, shook like jelly. The intensity and duration of the tremor was such that many of us thought Tokyo would collapse. But fortunately there were no serious consequences here.

Chaos ensued after the explosions at the Fukushima Daiichi Nuclear Power Plant, about a hundred miles from Tokyo. We didn't know if the whole of Tokyo would have to be evacuated, supermarket shelves were becoming bare, the streets were half deserted because people were afraid to go out, there were aftershocks keeping us awake at night . . . all these events piled up in the Tokyo psyche like a black cloud clinging to the top of a mountain.

That week after the disaster is seared into my memory. Ever since then I've been much more aware of the risk involved in living in a place that at any moment can be struck by Poseidon's trident.

A year later we visited Fukushima and Miyagi prefectures. We hired a car and after driving for three hours we began to notice changes in the landscape. We saw abandoned houses, supermarkets and gas stations overrun by vegetation like scenes from a post-apocalyptic movie or video game. The closer we got to the coast, the more half-destroyed houses and overturned cars we saw.

We stopped to look at one of the houses. We could see the interior

from outside as all the windows had gone. In another house we noticed that although the ground floor was devastated, the fixtures and fittings on the upstairs floor were undamaged, giving us an idea of how high the waters of the tsunami had reached. Most striking was that no one had touched a thing in this house since the incident. The television was still there, as were the beds, the family wardrobes with clothes spilling out of drawers, a karaoke machine, a laserdisc player.

Even a year after the tsunami and earthquake, scenes of desolation like the abandoned restaurant above, and the destroyed car below, were common.

MAGICAL MOMENTS
Crossing Matsushima Bridge

The vermilion of the bridge contrasted with the calm greenish blue of the sea, whose pacific waters lived up to the ocean's name. As we crossed the bridge to the island of Fukuurajima we were serenaded by the birdsong we could hear coming from the trees we were heading toward. An old man in a hat who'd obviously made an earlier start than us said hello as he passed us and carried on with his walk.

We wandered through the woods on Fukuurajima as the mist evaporated and the first rays of sunlight pierced the green canopy.

The calm of that morning, compared to the devastation we'd seen on our drive up here, brought it strongly home to me that nature is capable of creating serene beauty, but also has a destructive power we must never forget.

The magic of a place is often in the details. What is it that makes Japanese bridges so photogenic and gives the sensation that they're floating between the water and the sky? Look at the shape and the colors: they're simple, but unique. Would anyone use that shade of red to paint a bridge in the West?

A house destroyed by the tsunami that struck the region of Tohoku in 2011.

Pictures still hung on mud-splattered walls. The scene was mind-boggling. The tsunami took with it the life of the house while simultaneously freezing it in time.

We carried on northwards until we came across a railway station in ruins next to an entire town which had been abandoned. The streets were incredible, strewn with wrecked cars covered in vegetation.

We continued to explore the coastal towns we passed through until we arrived at the boundary of the exclusion zone around the Fukushima Daiichi Nuclear Power Plant. From that point on we weren't allowed any further because radiation levels were still too high. To get to the town of Matsushima, where we'd booked a ryokan for the night, we had to turn back and take an inland route.

After waking up the next morning in Matsushima, we went for a walk as a peaceful dawn broke. We took photos of the town's famous bridge surrounded by the still sea. Fortunately this area had suffered little damage, as the gulf it sits on had diluted the impact of the tsunami.

After our morning walk we went back to the car and headed for the small city of Kesennuma, along roads that led us through more ghost towns. In some of them, the only structures left standing were the gravestones.

Why does Japan have so many statues?

In Japan you find statues, figures and miniature shrines in forests, on roadsides, inside houses, in the middle of cities . . . Why?

Let's try to answer this question through the Prism of Natural Disasters (see chapter 2). The common feature of these symbols is they tend to survive any natural disaster. Books, buildings, human life: these can be destroyed. But a stone statue is likely to survive.

In a society that suffers from a cycle of destruction, it's important to have symbols that are difficult to destroy in order to preserve popular memory down the generations.

For example, in 1498 a tsunami flattened the city of Kamakura, near Tokyo, causing thousands of deaths and wiping out collective memories. Written records of every type were destroyed; one of the few things left was the statue of the Great Buddha of Kamakura. The Buddha's head had fallen to the ground, but it was repaired. This statue was one of the few things in Kamakura that survived this natural disaster.

In a society that is prone to natural disasters, it is important to have symbols that are immune to destruction.

In Kesennuma, whole neighborhoods had turned into wasteland. We came across a huge ship that had been dragged half a mile (750 meters) inland by the tsunami and ended up beached across a road, a reminder of the tsunami's power.

This 330 ton ship is named Kyotoku-maru No. 18 (第18共徳丸). The names of all Japanese ships end in *maru* 丸, which literally means "circle." It is said that *maru* symbolizes leaving the port, traveling the seas and coming home safe, thus completing a circle. It is also said that the suffix *maru* is used because Hakudo Maru is the name of the god who taught the Japanese people how to build boats.

The Kyotoku-maru No. 18 ended up trapped on land, unable to complete its circle. Some residents of Kesennuma suggested building a park around it and turning it into a World Heritage Site to commemorate the disaster. But after much deliberation, the citizens decided they wanted to remove it from the landscape. According to the victims of the tsunami, it was an obstacle to the rebuilding of the town and they considered it more of a scar than a memorial.

Years later, a Japanese theater director called me to ask if he could use one of my photographs of the Kyotoku-maru No. 18 in one of his new plays. The photograph was projected onto the stage backdrop and was also used as the main image on the tickets. The play ran for months at the National Theater of Japan. The profits raised were donated

to help with the continuing reconstruction of the areas that had been devastated by the tsunami.

In the months and years following the catastrophe, practically all the people of Japan helped with the recovery in one way or another. Even today, ten years later, we pay a special tax that is used to carry on rebuilding the devastated areas.

Helping and collaborating with people, even when they're strangers, is something which joins people to each other through the spirit of *kizuna* 絆. The left-hand element of the Japanese character for the word kizuna represents "string" or "thread," and the whole word means something like "family ties," but goes beyond the idea of the family. Kizuna implies a connection between all of us. Kizuna could be described as an invisible thread that unites all human beings and also all elements of nature. The word encourages the kind of collective action that is essential in helping communities recover from disaster.

Experiencing this disaster has helped me to understand the Japanese psyche more profoundly. Now when I notice an aversion to risk in Japanese people, I don't get annoyed by what I once might have perceived as a lack of courage. I simply look at it through the Prism of Natural Disasters and I feel more empathy for the way they act.

The same thing happens when I realize I'm being too individualistic or selfish; I'm inspired by the collaborative spirit of kizuna and I choose to prioritize others over myself.

I say to myself that I'm not alone here but rather that we're all in this together. I try to remember that when all is said and done we're all passengers on this gigantic ball we call planet Earth as it hurtles through the universe, and no one knows when nature will decide to do away with us. Thoughts like these help me to put my ego to one side and to think about not only my own life, but the whole of humanity, from a more liberating perspective.

When we visited Kesennuma, the streets had been cleared of debris. All that was left was the ship, Kyotoku-maru No. 18.

An Eyewitness Account of the 1923 Great Kanto Earthquake

The Spanish novelist Vicente Blasco Ibáñez visited Yokohama just after the 1923 Great Kanto Earthquake, which destroyed both Yokohama and neighboring Tokyo. In his book *Japón* (Japan), he made the following observations:

I saw Reims after several months of bombardment; during the last war I visited towns that had been systematically destroyed by the German invasion; but the horror of this enormous city shaken to its foundations by the trembling of the ground and consumed then by flames, is much more moving and painful. Man, with all his scientific wickedness, could not match in years the destructive power that unconscious nature can unleash in a matter of minutes [. . .]

Nothing breaks the horizon vertically, not one tower, not one two-story house. Everything is demolished. No building manages to exceed human height. Walls scorched by fire, looking like nothing more than simple barriers, are pointed out by travelers who knew Yokohama before the earthquake. There stood the big banks, the multistory department stores that had been built in the image of New York. There stood the hotels that offered levels of comfort equal to the most famous palaces.

Niijima Island

Niijima is a volcanic island off the coast of Tokyo. Local legend has it that Niijima was created after an earthquake in 1703, and prior to that Niijima and neighboring Shikinejima formed a single island. Hence the name Niijima, "new island" (新 new; 島 island). The volcanic nature of the island makes its topography spectacular: forests, mountains and deserted beaches combine with dramatic cliffs.

Even when it rains you won't get wet is the first thing I read on a poster when we disembark at Niijima ferry port, and we watch as the cloud of drizzle which seemed to be following our boat from Oshima, 大島 (大 big; 島 island) turns into a rainbow.

"Hi! Are you the people who are staying at the Fujiya guest house?" asks a trim, smiling woman of about fifty.

"Yes, that's us."

"My name's Michi. How was your journey? You must be tired . . ."

"It was long, but we slept most of the night."

"I'll take you to the guest house right away, it's five minutes by car," says Michi as she opens the trunk of the car for our backpacks.

We head toward the guest house along a road next to the ocean. We pass under another cloud that sprinkles the car with rain for a few seconds.

"The good thing about driving on Niijima is that there isn't a single traffic light on the whole island," Michi says with a certain pride as she looks at me out of the corner of her eye; I'm in the passenger seat. "And do you know the best thing of all? You can park anywhere," she says, knowing how difficult it is to find a parking space in the center of Tokyo.

The woman who greets us with a smile at the door of the guest house must be Michi's mother. She looks about eighty, but moves around with the agility of a cat. She opens the door to our room and before we've even had time to take off our backpacks she asks: "Have you come here to go surfing?"

"We've come just to visit the island."

"Most of the young people who come to Niijima are here for the surfing," she replies, unfolding a couple of maps on the table.

"We've come to see unusual things . . . Can you tell us where the missile launch platform is?" I ask, having read earlier that the island is a strategic location for the protection of Tokyo. Following the territorial dispute between Japan and China over the ownership of the Senkaku Islands off the coast of Taiwan, we're all a lot better informed about these matters.

"The missile launchers are in the south, but I don't know exactly where," she says, bringing the map closer to her eyes.

I start to look at the maps on my smartphone but absolutely nothing appears in the south of the island. It's not on her map either, but she concludes with some conviction: "I'm sure it's in the south-west. You should go in the morning, the sunrise from there is beautiful."

The next day we get up at three thirty in the morning and head south. We cross the town of Honson, one of Niijima's two towns and immediately we're on the only road south, narrow and dark beneath overhanging branches. We go slowly, we have plenty of time to find the military zone from where we'll have good views of the dawn, which will

FACING PAGE Sunrise over Niijima.
LEFT Waiting for dawn. Even though you're still within the municipal district of Tokyo, you can enjoy the starry skies.
BELOW One of the moai-style statues that can be found on Niijima.

four hours. Each day, when we get tired of running around, usually at sunset, we sit and soak for hours. Bathing in volcanic waters while enjoying the ocean breeze is a wonderful experience.

On the last day we get into Michi's car. Her mother runs out to the street to say goodbye, with her usual smile. She waves goodbye tirelessly, her arm moving from side to side, until we start to go round the first bend and lose sight of her.

"My mother's been running the guest house for forty-six years but every day is like the first day for her," says Michi.

At the port, as we wait for the ferry, I read the sign again:

Ame ga futtemo nurenaizo
雨が降っても濡れないぞう
Even when it rains you won't get wet
— *Niijima Island saying*

As I read it, I smile. Now I understand perfectly. It rained on two of the three days we spent here, but not for a moment did we need an umbrella as the rain was merely drizzle, which, as the sign boasts, doesn't really get you very wet.

start to break at five o'clock. We reach the end of the road and we're on a clifftop. It's still dark and our only light is from the stars. We sit and watch as the black sky slowly brightens with the dawn.

We've found part of the military installation, although it doesn't appear to be the launch area. It's the power station which supplies energy to the missile launch platform and to the civilians who live on the island.

We carry on the search along a minor road but arrive again at a gate with a sign saying: 技術研究本部 航空装備研究所新島支所, 防衛庁, which translates as "Equipment Research and Development Center of the Niijima Air Force, Ministry of Defence." At the other side of the fence you can see a couple of hangars and two or three trucks surrounded by woods. I hope it's always a research centre and that they never have to use it to launch missiles.

We conclude that this is surely all we'll be able to see of the military installation and we set off in search of our next objective: to find the moai statues on the island. They are similar to those on Easter Island but much smaller. There are quite a few moai on Niijima, sculpted by an artist who lives two streets up from our guest house in Honson.

We spend several days exploring every corner of the island. The best thing was our daily open-air bath at the *onsen* hot spring, which is open twenty-

Gunma: Snow Country

Gunma Prefecture, north of Tokyo is a favorite escape for Tokyo residents looking to escape the stress of the city and enjoy the *onsen* hot springs at the weekends.

I've been to Gunma several times, to enjoy walking in nature, eating well and soaking in volcanic waters. Having seen Gunma in spring and in summer, it wasn't until I went there in the middle of winter that I fell completely in love with the place.

When the white of the snow covers the region and you go deeper along the roads that follow the course of crystal clear rivers through steep valleys, you feel as though you're traveling in another dimension. Yasunari Kawabata's famous novel *Snow Country* Yukiguni 雪国 (雪 snow; 国 country) is set in Gunma Prefecture, and it opens with the following evocative lines: "The train came out of

the long tunnel into the snow country. The land was white under the night sky."

At the car-hire office near Minakami Station, the car they give us is already fitted with snow chains. Driving in snowy conditions isn't a pleasant experience, as the edges of the road are difficult to see. The closer we get to our destination, the higher the banks of snow on both sides of the road. The posts indicating the snow levels and the limit of the asphalt can barely be seen.

We arrive at Takaragawa Onsen, a hot-springs ryokan consisting of a group of traditional buildings imaginatively assembled along the banks of a river.

We park and cross a wooden footbridge. There's not a soul around, it's snowing heavily, and it's so foggy we can barely see the river as it runs below us. The bridge is arched slightly and as we get to the middle of it, we start to be able to make out the entrance to the hotel, where a group of snow-cov-

The mountains of Gunma Prefecture are covered in thick snow for much of the winter, making you feel as though you've traveled to a different dimension.

ered *tanuki* raccoon-dog statues guard the door.

We are shown to our room, which has a view over the river as it runs through the snow. It's still too early for dinner, so we decide to take a hot-spring bath.

Usually in Japan, hot-spring bathing is segregated by sex, but here it's an *onsen konyoku*, which means that men and women share the same bath. You have to go in naked, but there are certain rules and etiquette. If you're a man, you have to try to cover your private parts with the small towel provided. Women are given a larger towel to cover the chest area downward.

There are several baths of different sizes and varying temperatures, allowing you to choose the one you like most. Some of the baths are covered to prevent the cold snow from falling on your head but the majority are open-air baths, known as *rotenburo* in Japanese.

We enter the largest rotenburo in the complex, which turns out to hold the national record for the largest onsen bath in Japan. There are twenty or so people bathing, all sitting calmly like monkeys

温泉 Onsen

Onsen 温泉 (温 hot; 泉 source, spring) are areas of volcanic hot springs. They are found practically everywhere in Japan..

For a spring to be classed as an onsen, the water must be strictly volcanic in origin. If not, it's classed as a spa. According to Japanese government statistics there were 27, 422 onsen in Japan as of 2016.

There are many types of onsen, classified according to the minerals the water contains and the curative properties they have.

Here are some useful words to know when you're visiting an onsen:

Rotenburo 露天風呂: open air bath.

Naiyu 内湯: bath inside a building or a house.

Konyoku 混浴: onsen in which men and women bathe together.

How to identify onsen on signs and maps:

■ From the complete word onsen: 温泉.

■ From the symbol ♨ (also used in Korea).

■ From the characters 湯 or ゆ (meaning "hot water"). If you only see one of the characters it might not be an onsen, but perhaps a *sento* (neighborhood public bath) or a spa.

Heavy snow covers a traditional Japanese ryokan inn and its gardens.

relaxing. I approach the rocky edge of the bath aware that if I slip, I risk falling into the river's almost freezing water. Snowflakes fall on my head and shoulders incessantly.

Imitating everyone else, I lower myself into the water and sit with my knees placed so that I can rest my chin on them.

A dense fog further smudges the landscape whose contours have already been blurred by snow. I look around me and apart from the white shape of the mountain and the baths on either side of the river, I can hardly see anything. In the distance I can make out the bridge we crossed when we came into the hotel, but nothing beyond it. Under the trees I spot the shadowy shapes of a few *toro* traditional stone lanterns.

People bathe in silence; all you can hear is the rushing water of the river. Steam rises from the volcanic waters as if the heat from within the mountain is battling against the cold of the snow. When I start to feel too hot, I move to another pool where the water's a little cooler.

"Where are you from?" asks one of my fellow bathers, a woman who has kindly made the effort to speak in English.

"*Supein, demo, Tokio ni sunde imasu* [Spain, but I live in Tokyo]."

"*Ahhh, so desu ka!* [Wow, incredible!]," she says in Japanese, realizing that I understand it.

Another two women next to her can't help but respond in surprise and they whisper "*Sugoi na, koko made kite* [Amazing that he's come to such an inhospitable place]."

"Do you like onsen?"

"I love them."

The three of them laugh as if I've said something funny. The conversation catches the attention of a man who's bathing with a little white towel covering his bald head, half dozing with his eyes closed. He opens them, perhaps we're bothering him, but it turns out we're not; he's interested and begins to listen more closely.

"Why do you like onsen?" asks the woman.

"I like the feeling of being completely naked and

in direct contact with nature," I tell her.

"*Ah, so desu ka* (That's what it's like, isn't it?) And don't you like the way it leaves your skin feeling so soft?"

The other two women lift their arms out of the water and brush their skin as if to demonstrate the rejuvenating powers of the water. As we speak, the snowflakes keep falling, disappearing as they touch our skin or the waters of the bath.

"And also, this onsen has some of the best waters in Gunma for rheumatism," adds the man.

"Hey, you know a lot, are you from the area?" one of the women asks him.

"No, I'm from Saitama but I come here specifically for the waters," the man replies. "I've not been sleeping well lately because of my rheumatism . . ."

"The onsen is our doctor for lots of things," the woman says to me. She says it with pride, as though trying to explain to me something good about Japan.

The man with the towel moves closer to us, trying to grab our attention:

"Did you know that you used to be able to bathe with bears here?"

After this rhetorical question he expands on his subject, telling us in detail how one of the main attractions of this onsen in the past was that people could bathe with tame bears. It turns out that a change in Japanese law around the treatment of animals brought an end to the practice.

In the onsen, the Japanese tend to be more outgoing than usual, I'd even say extrovert. Almost as much as when they've had a few too many beers. So don't be surprised if someone strikes up a conversation with you when you're taking an onsen bath.

We decide that we'll venture to the other side of the river to try some other baths – crossing the wooden footbridge wearing nothing but a towel! The winter wind is freezing, but when you've been soaking for a good while in steaming hot water, your body doesn't seem to notice.

After bathing in a couple more baths we go back to have dinner in the restaurant of the ryokan. One of the peculiarities of the traditional *kaiseki* multi-course dinner is that the usual miso soup is replaced by bear-meat soup.

The sensation of eating after a couple of hours of soaking your body in thermal water as the snow falls around you is magnificent. My mind is calm and I feel reborn. Nothing worries me.

The next day, the snowfall has abated and over the mountains there are patches of blue sky between the clouds. They serve us a breakfast of wild mushrooms and local vegetables and another bowl of bear-meat soup.

I sit for a few moments staring through the window next to our breakfast table. It's a beautiful landscape, but at the same time a desolate one. I imagine how solitary life must be for the locals who have to spend the whole winter here. I picture Shimamura, Komako and Yoko, the main characters in Kawabata's *Snow Country*, trapped forever in this place of solitude.

Nichitsu Ghost Town

Nichitsu Ghost Town is one of the most spectacular *haikyo* 廃墟 (abandoned places) in Japan.

It's close to the center of the main island of Honshu, where the prefectures of Gunma, Saitama and Nagano meet and is a place that few people know about. To get there, we hired a car and set off early in the morning.

We drove up mountain roads above narrow river valleys. After an hour or so, other traffic disappeared and it seemed as if the mountains were going to swallow up the road we were traveling along. Our trepidation grew. The final tunnel we went through was barely wide enough for one vehicle. We could see nothing but darkness and the distant white light of the exit. Coming out of the tunnel we caught our first sight of the buildings of Nichitsu, a town that was abandoned when the local mine closed down.

The town had lived thanks to mining. Gold had been mined there since the year 1600 and later, zinc and iron. In 1937 the mines were bought by the Nichitsu Corporation, hence the name of the town.

In 1978, the workers and their families began to leave the town as the mines' reserves started to run out. Nobody has lived there for decades.

Even so, as we walked through the streets we got the feeling that people could have been living there as recently as a month ago. Lots of things were still intact. We visited the theater, the public baths, which in the past would have been full of *onsen* hot-spring water, a hospital with a fully equipped operating room, the homes where the miners and their families used to sleep . . .

In the rooms of abandoned houses we saw magazines from the time, board games, cutlery sets, bed that were still covered in blankets and sheets. There were still canned goods on the supermarket shelves. It's a town which would be perfect for shooting a movie about zombies or some post-apocalyptic catastrophe.

Nichitsu is a disturbing place that made me reflect on the past and the future. It struck me deeply how our living conditions and our fates can change from one day to the next without warning.

軍艦島 Battleship Island

Nichitsu isn't an exception. In areas far away from the big cities there are more and more locations that are classed as *haikyo* (abandoned places).

Gunkanjima is perhaps the best-known haikyo. It's a small island in Nagasaki Prefecture. The whole island was bought by Mitsubishi in 1890 when they discovered coal reserves under the sea. Gunkanjima 軍艦島 literally means "battleship island" because the shape of the island brings to mind a battleship.

The tiny sixteen-acre (six-hectare) island was initially populated by a small group of workers, but in time the population grew until it became the most densely populated location in the world with a population of over 5,000 people in 1959. To cater to the growing population, apartment blocks, cinemas, recreation centers, casinos, swimming pools and supermarkets were built, all of which are now only inhabited by seagulls and rats.

In 1974 the coal ran out and Mitsubishi officially announced the closure of its undersea coal mines around Gunkanjima. Since then it's been a ghost island: nobody has lived there since 1975. It went from being the area with the highest population density in the world to being uninhabited.

In 2002 Mitsubishi decided to donate the island to the city of Nagasaki and since 2009 certain parts of the island can be visited; before then access was restricted to historians and journalists. A return ticket by ferry from the port of Nagasaki costs ¥4,500.

FAR LEFT A magazine from the 1970s lies on the floor of an abandoned house.
LEFT, TOP Taking pictures from outside: it's too dangerous to go in.
LEFT, BOTTOM The remains of a former financial institution.
ABOVE, TOP An abandoned supermarket.
ABOVE An abandoned hospital.

Niigata Prefecture

Niigata Prefecture is situated on a plain stretching between the Japanese Alps and the Sea of Japan. In winter the climate is severe and heavy snow covers the landscape.

I'd passed through once on the way to the city of Kanazawa and another time I'd stayed at an *onsen* hot-spring inn deep in the snowy mountains on the border of Gunma and Niigata prefectures.

But after fourteen years in Japan I still didn't know the area, so I chose it as a destination to explore for a few days.

At the station in Tokyo we got on the Niigata bullet train, the Joetsu Shinkansen. The unusual thing about this bullet train is that there are several double-decker models; if you want good views, choose a seat on the upper deck when you book. Although a large part of the journey is spent in tunnels crossing the mountains of the Japanese Alps, the views crossing Gunma and into Niigata are impressive.

Barely two hours after leaving Tokyo we reached Niigata Station and stepped out into this city of eight hundred thousand inhabitants.

The main exit from the station (called the Bandai exit) leads into a big, ugly square, surrounded by buildings that look as if they were designed by a Soviet town planner from the early twentieth century. What saves the square and gives it some

character is the fact that each of the facades of the buildings is covered in neon signs.

We checked into our hotel near the station, dumped our luggage and went out to eat.

We found a restaurant serving *teishoku* 定食 set meals, and we stuffed ourselves. Outside Tokyo, restaurant prices are cheaper and portions are more generous. For barely ¥800, I wolfed down a meal of two enormous grilled mackerel (*saba*) with rice and miso soup .

The next day we took the ferry to Sado Island. A flock of seagulls, encouraged by a group of children throwing bread to them, accompanied us from the port to the open sea.

The topography of Sado Island, with steep mountains in the north and plains in the south,

ABOVE The Joetsu Shinkansen.
LEFT At the entrance to the gold mine, surrounded by old people making us feel young.
RIGHT, TOP Niigata Prefecture has spectacular mountain scenery.
RIGHT, BOTTOM A traditional Sado Island *tarai bune* boat.

makes it an ideal place to grow rice for making sake. The locals explained this fact to us with pride, claiming that they produced some of the best sake in Japan.

We started our exploration of the island in the mountains, which offer spectacular views not just of the natural scenery but of a gigantic military radar station on one of the summits. As it happens, Sado Island is one of the closest places in the country to North Korea.

On our way down toward the sea we stopped to visit what was the most productive gold mine in Japan during the Edo period (1603–1868). It's been made into a museum open to tourists, where you can get an idea of how hard it was to be a miner on Sado Island. Most of people who worked in these

mines had been sent by the shogunate as a punishment, which gave the island a reputation as a place of exile.

After visiting the mine we reached the west coast, where there's an area of strangely shaped coral reefs, and fishing ports. We sailed along the coast in a little fishing boat, enjoying the sunset, and we were lucky enough to see a *toki* — a species of ibis which thrives in the local climate and feeds at the edges of the rice fields. The toki is the mascot of Sado Island.

The population of Sado is falling and many of those who live there are elderly. Young people leave the island as soon as they can to work in the big cities, which is a source of worry for the local community.

Ibaraki and Mito

Ibaraki, to the north of Tokyo, is one of the prefectures with the least tourism. That's precisely why I decide to go there.

We travel by train to the main station in Mito, the prefectural capital, and head for our hotel, a ten-minute taxi ride away. The hotel staff greet us with bows as we step out of the taxi. After checking in, we're informed that the hotel bar is offering *nomihodai* (all you can drink for a fixed price), so we spend some time there before dinner.

We soon realize we're the only guests in the hotel. It doesn't seem to be a tourist hotel; the second floor has no bedrooms, only function rooms. When the sun goes down, we spot a crowd gathering on the second floor; it turns out the local basketball team is having a party to celebrate the beginning of the season.

During our first two days here we explore the legacy of Tokugawa Nariaki, one of the last daimyo feudal lords to govern Mito Province (present-day Ibaraki Prefecture).

Mito Castle was built in the thirteenth century and was be held by the Tokugawa clan from 1603 onward. Tokugawa Nariaki (1800–1860), was interested in culture and established a school for nobles and high-ranking samurai, the Kodokan, which was dedicated to the study of Japanese history and religion.

The school based its philosophy on Neo-Confucianism, which represented a vision opposed to the Buddhist thinking of the period. According to Buddhism and also Taoism, the universe isn't real since all its elements move from not existing to existing and vice versa. Neo-Confucianism uses the path of reason to explain the nature of things and insists on their "true" existence.

The Kodokan was one of the first schools in Japan to start observing nature through the lens of reason. Little by little, in addition to the subjects of history and religion, the school also started to

LEFT The platform of Oarai train station.
RIGHT The architecture of the Kobuntei blends perfectly with the surrounding gardens.

devote time to the study of astronomy, medicine and natural sciences.

We visit the Kodokan, which is separated from the rest of the city by a small wall about eight feet (2.5 meters) high. We buy our tickets and go into the grounds, where only two hundred years ago several hundred men would have been exercising their minds and their bodies.

After strolling through the gardens, we prepare to enter the school by taking off our shoes and putting them into a plastic bag. (Don't forget to take your shoes off whenever you go into a traditional house or building in Japan.)

Once inside we walk through the rooms where students once slept, meditated, and studied, decorated today like a museum with parchment paintings of scenes from the period and books of poetry written by the students.

Besides the Kodokan, another important legacy of Tokugawa Nariaki, in honor of the beauty of nature, is the Kairakuen gardens.

As an admirer of Confucius, Tokugawa Nariaki liked to apply his teachings whenever he could. At the beginning of his notes ordering the construction of both the Kodokan and the Kairakuen gardens, Nariaki wrote, "Tension is as important as relaxation," using the exact words found in the *Book of Rites* by Confucius. According to Confucius, in addition to living intensely, we also need to relax in order to lead a good life. For Tokugawa Nariaki, the building of the Kodokan represented tension, whereas the Kairakuen gardens were dedicated to relaxation.

At one of the highest points of the gardens Tokugawa Nariaki built a three-story house called Kobuntei which he used for rest days and also for throwing parties with his friends. This house is open to the public and is one of the places with the best views of the park.

You can also visit all the rooms in the house. On the third floor is a function room from which you can see Mount Fuji on clear days. This was Tokugawa Nariaki's favorite room and in it he hung a parchment with one of his most-loved passages from Confucius:

Wise people enjoy water,
People of virtue enjoy the mountains.
Wise people move,
People of virtue stay still.
Wise people love themselves,
People of virtue celebrate the lives of everyone else.

The gardens also have a plum orchard that is beautiful when the trees blossom in mid-February, the time when most visitors come to the gardens.

We leave Kairakuen and continue our walk, visiting the nearby shrine of Tokiwa Jinja and then we cross a small bamboo forest to get to a spring where water emerges from a large white rock. At dusk we walk through a field of poppies on the way back to the hotel.

The next day we decide to visit the Ibaraki coast. We board a local train, and after traveling through six miles (ten kilometers) of rice fields, we reach the coastal town of Oarai. From the station we take a bus to the beach, which we walk along to get to our destination: Oarai Isosaki Shrine, with its distinctive *torii* gate that seems to be floating on the sea.

Although the best views are at sunrise when, depending on the time of year, you can see the ball of the sun emerge above the ocean behind the torii, we enjoyed a sunset which, if not so spectacular, was wonderful all the same.

LEFT The gardens of Kairakuen were one of the legacies of the daimyo Tokugawa Nariaki.
ABOVE Oarai Isosaki Shrine has a distinctive *torii* gate that seems to float on the sea.

大名 Daimyo

Daimyo 大名 (大 great; 名 private land) was the title used for the regional rulers of Japan from the tenth century until the year 1868.

The daimyo had a certain amount of independence in the government of their provinces but they all had to answer to the shogun, the person with absolute power over the whole of Japan.

When the shogun Tokugawa Ieyasu came to power in 1603, marking the start of the Edo period, he ordered a reorganization of the almost two hundred daimyo who controlled each of the provinces (*han*). The level of power of each daimyo was classified according to the quantity of rice each province was able to produce in a year. Tokugawa Ieyasu ordered the removal of daimyo status from those who were unable to produce at least ten thousand *koku* annually. The koku is a unit of measurement of rice approximately equivalent to the amount necessary to feed one person for a year.

MY TRAVEL TIPS

Japan's Three Famous Gardens: The Nihon Sanmeien

Nihon Sanmeien 日本三名園 means "the three biggest and most famous gardens in Japan." I've already introduced Kairakuen in Mito (see page 162); the other two are Korakuen in Okayama Prefecture and Kenrokuen in the city of Kanazawa.

ABOVE Kenrokuen 兼六園 in Kanazawa. The name means "garden of the six features," referring to the six aspects considered most important when it comes to designing a garden: serenity and isolation, respect for ancestors, beautiful views from nearly every spot, coolness (requiring the flow of water), attention to detail and spaciousness. BELOW Korakuen 後楽園 in Okayama. Japanese-style gardens are often designed to emulate real landscapes in smaller dimensions. Korakuen has water channels that symbolize rivers, and mounds fifteen to thirty feet (five to ten meters) high that represent mountains.

Miyajima

Miyajima 宮島, also known as Itsukushima 厳島, is a small island near Hiroshima, famous for the beauty of its landscapes, where shrine buildings blend with nature. The whole island is regarded as sacred territory; its very name says it all (Miya 宮: sacred temple; jima 島: island). Many gods inhabit the island and it is believed that the island itself is a *kami* (god or spirit).

No births or deaths are allowed on the island, nor is it permitted to cut down trees or kill animals. These rules have encouraged hundreds of monkeys and deer to live freely on the island. Deer, according to Shinto tradition, are messengers of the gods.

The island is home to Itsukushima Shrine, a World Heritage Site, considered one of the most beautiful places in Japan and the world. It was built more than 1,500 years ago and has been rebuilt several times. The loveliest aspect of the shrine is the enormous *torii* gate, which can be reached on foot at low tide, and whose reflection can be seen in the water when the tide comes in. This torii gate is one of the best-known images of Japan.

In the past people weren't even allowed to set foot on the island, which is why the buildings of Itsukushima Shrine are elevated above the sea water on a beach, like a jetty. Access to the island only used to be permitted on a small boat which passed through the torii shrine gate so as to be cleansed before arriving in sacred territory. The "floating" torii gate is fifty-two feet (sixteen meters) high and its posts are all made from the trunk of the same tree. The gate has several reinforcement columns so it can withstand storms and even typhoons.

Two other important temples on the island are Toyokuni and Senjokaku, a temple and a five-story pagoda respectively. They were built by daimyo

Itsukushima Shrine, a World Heritage Site, is widely considered one of the most beautiful places in Japan.

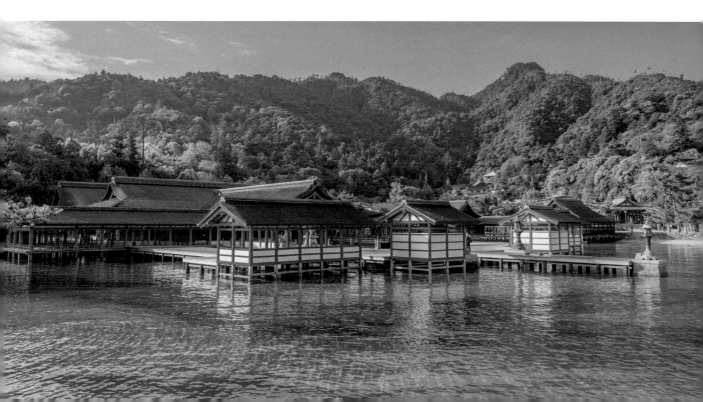

MAGICAL DETAILS
Miyajima

The traditional way of serving white rice in Japan is to use a wooden spoon called a *shakushi*. It is said that if you use a spoon that isn't made of wood it changes the flavor of the rice. Legend has it that the first shakushi spoon was invented by a monk from Miyajima. Consequently, one of the most popular souvenirs in the island's stores are wooden shakushi spoons.

There are no road signs on Miyajima Island. Only two thousand people live there and the roads are virtually free from traffic.

A Miyajima superstition says that if you throw a stone and you manage to land it right on the frame of the famous red *torii* gate you can make a wish and it will be granted. But if you hit a stone that somebody else put there before you, your wish won't come true, and in fact you will be the receiver of bad luck.

If you have the chance to walk out to the torii gate at low tide you'll notice all the stones on the supporting frames between the main columns.

Visitors can walk to the *torii* gate of Itsukushima Shrine at low tide.

Miyajima is one of the most photogenic places in Japan. Book your visit well in advance as it's a very small island with a limited number of ferries and hotels.

Toyotomi Hideyoshi, regarded as the unifier of Japan, at the end of the sixteenth century. He built them to honor the spirits of those who'd given their lives in the war to unify Japan. The best time to visit the temple and pagoda is the cherry blossom season. Seeing the pagoda surrounded by flowers is wonderful.

The summit of Mount Misen is the highest point on the island. You can go up on foot or by cable car (open from 9 a.m. to 5 p.m.). It's worth walking up, as among other things you'll see monkeys and young deer in the maple forests, which are especially pretty in autumn when they're tinged with shades of orange. There are three main routes:

- **The Momijidani trail:** this is the busiest of the three routes. At the start is the Shinomiya temple, where you can enjoy tea in a traditional tea house. A little higher up you can board the cable car.
- **The Daisho-in trail:** the most interesting thing is the Daisho-in Buddhist temple, right at the beginning of the route. The Dalai Lama himself has visited it. You can visit the Daisho-in temple and then take another trail to the top.
- **The Ornoto trail:** the least well-known of the three routes but to me it seems the most magical, perhaps because it's the quietest. Start just behind Ornoto Shrine.

Near the summit there are several small temples; one of them is Gumonjido, which has a lighted candle that is said to have been alight continuously since the ninth century when the temple was built. From the summit there's a panoramic view of Miyajima and also of the surrounding islands.

How to Get There

The most convenient way is to take the JR Sanyo train from Hiroshima to Miyami-guchi Station. The ferry terminal is next to the station and the ferry runs from 6 a.m. to 10 p.m.
Best Time to Visit You can see the island comfortably in a day, and quickly in an afternoon. But it's such an idyllic spot that it's best to see it in a calm, relaxed way. When I've gone there I've always spent the night on the island and had two days to enjoy the scenery. The advantage of staying overnight is that you get to experience the island empty of daytrippers. Walking the quiet streets in the early morning or seeing Itsukushima Shrine lit up at night are both extraordinary experiences. If you want a hotel on the island, book one several months in advance, as they are very popular.

Hakone

The first time I went to Hakone it was raining and I wasn't able to see Mount Fuji over Lake Ashi.

The second time, I went to Hakone with my parents who were visiting from Spain. I booked three nights at a ryokan facing Mount Fuji. As we were walking along the shore of the lake on the first night I said to them: "If we're here for three days I'm sure we'll get a sight of it."

Each morning I woke at dawn, looking forward to seeing the iconic peak. My eyes full of sleep, I went out into the garden of the ryokan in my *yukata* dressing gown to check if I was in luck. But Mount

Fuji and all the other mountains and forests around us were covered in a veil of mist that seemed to come straight out of an Oscar Wilde novel.

We left Hakone without seeing Mount Fuji.

I eventually learned that Mount Fuji reveals itself when you least expect it; sometimes it's shy and other times it's shameless. In the winter months, its snowy peak greets me almost every morning when I look out of my Tokyo office window. But in summer it abandons the people of Tokyo, hidden in the haze, occasionally appearing after a storm or typhoon has cleared the air.

On my sixth visit to Hakone my expectations were very low. As soon as I got off the bus, still sleepy and a bit dizzy after half an hour of twisting mountain roads, I went into a convenience store to get myself a coffee without even glancing at the scenery.

"Daddy, look, you can see Mount Fuji," said a child looking through the store window. I turned towards the window while I waited for the coffee machine to finish, and there it was.

I sat down to drink my coffee by Lake Ashi. I was joined by several fishermen who put down their rods and picked up their smartphones to take as many photos as they could because they knew the spectacle wouldn't last. The clouds arrived straight away and began to enfold the base of the majestic mountain, leaving the summit floating in the sky. In a matter of minutes the clouds had covered the mountain completely and taken it off into another dimension.

I walked toward Moto-Hakone pier and there I came across Mr. Casca and Ms. Wonder, involved in an argument:

"What a joke these pirate boats are!" said Mr. Casca, roaring with laughter.

"Stop laughing and try to show some respect. They're *kawaii* and the children love them," replied Ms. Wonder.

"They're horrible – the scenery is perfect and the boats ruin your photos. They look like bad-taste stickers," said Mr. Casca, and he carried on laughing as he watched one of the pirate ships docking at the quayside.

I got on the boat with Mr. Casca and Ms. Wonder to cross to the other side of the lake. As we sailed, the views seemed to calm Mr. Casca, who stopped complaining. Mount Fuji appeared again for a few moments, and Mr. Casca asked me to take a photo of the two of them with Fuji in the background. It was the last time Mount Fuji was visible that day.

After leaving the pirate boat we took the Hakone Tozan cable car to the volcanic valley of Owakudani 大涌谷 (lit., the great valley that boils). Several barriers indicated the areas where it was forbidden to walk because it was too dangerous – most areas, it seemed. All around was stunted vegetation, yellowish colored soil and jets of water and steam spurting here and there.

I sat on a bench to watch the volcanic activity and eat a couple of black eggs boiled in volcanic water. Mr. Casca and Ms. Wonder sat on the bench next to me with their own little bag of black eggs.

"It stinks of sulphur!" Mr. Casca complained.

This time Ms. Wonder didn't respond and I too agreed in silence. Even in the open air, the stench was intense, unpleasant and impossible to ignore. I ate my second hard-boiled egg and left for Tokyo.

FACING PAGE Hakone is famous for its five lakes, the best-known of which is Lake Ashi.
ABOVE The Hakone Tozan cable car.
BELOW At the volcanic valley of Owakudani, visitors can boil eggs in the sulfuric waters.

The Izu Peninsula

Izu is a peninsula which forms part of Shizuoka Prefecture, south of Tokyo. With Mount Fuji watching over it to the north, and the sea surrounding it to the east, south and west, it is ideally placed to offer splendid views.

On our trip there, we decide to base ourselves in the city of Atami. This is one of the best-connected cities in Izu as it has a *shinkansen* bullet train station. We rent a house facing the sea and from there we choose a destination to explore each day.

Atami is a city whose tourist boom was in the 1970s and 1980s, during the Japanese economic bubble. Its beaches and ocean views attracted tourists from all over the country and from overseas too.

It's still a city whose economy is based on tourism, but it's not what it was. If Mr. Casca was walking around Atami, he would doubtless say to Ms. Wonder, "This city has an air of decay about it." The paintwork on the facades of some the buildings is peeling and some of its streets are not well looked after.

But in this case I'd prefer to think positively and to look at the world like Ms. Wonder, who would answer Mr. Casca by saying: "I like Atami, it has the whiff of Showa about it." (In Japanese they talk about those things which have hardly changed since the Showa era [1926–1989] as having the taste or smell of Showa.)

Both Mr. Casca and Ms. Wonder are correct. Atami has well cared for, retro corners which make you feel as though you're in the Japan of the past, but there are certain streets that look almost abandoned and have certainly seen better days.

The house we rent is big, with a strange mixture of Western and Eastern styles. It reminds me of the house where the main character lives in the novel *Killing Commendatore* by Haruki Murakami.

In the garden there's a *sakura* cherry tree that's just about to flower. From the large living-room window we can see a thin line of sea on the horizon and a grey blanket of low cloud casting a shadow over the landscape.

We have tea in the eight-mat tatami room next the living room. Outside, drops of rain start to fall on the sakura tree.

At the far end of the living-room is a grand piano with a bouquet of flowers and several volumes of manga on it. I play the piano for a while, accompanied by the pitter-patter of the rain and interrupted now and then by the rattle of the occasional passing train on the tracks that are just behind the house.

It's the line traveled by the train called the Izu Odoriko (The Dancing Girl of Izu), the same name as the story by Yasunari Kawabata (the first

The sea view after crossing the Kadowakitsuri Suspension Bridge on the Jogasaki coast.

The Kadowakitsuri Suspension Bridge. On a windy day the bridge will sway and crossing it will make you feel dizzy.

Japanese writer to win the Nobel Prize for Literature). In fact, the train was named after the novel.

In Kawabata's story, a young man from Tokyo is traveling around the Izu peninsula and one day happens upon a group of itinerant dancers who come from the nearby island of Oshima. He falls in love at first sight with the youngest girl in the group, who plays the drum and dances. At first he only watches her from afar. Later, when he comes across the dancers in a tea house, he strikes up a friendship with the only man in the group. He spends a few days traveling across Izu with the group of dancers, but his love for the girl is never consummated, it merely fuels his imagination. At the end of the story when he says goodbye to his new group of friends, he realizes at the last moment that they are leaving for different destinations, and that perhaps he will never see her, or the rest of the group, again. He returns to Tokyo and they go back to the island of Oshima.

Kawabata's story was so popular that later there were several movies entitled *The Dancing Girl of Izu*, as well as plays. There are even traditional *enka* songs dedicated to the love story portrayed in the novel.

On the second day of our trip, walking along the cliffs at Jogasaki, in the east of the peninsula, I stare at the unmistakable triangular shape of the island of Oshima, the very island that was the home of the dancers in the story by Kawabata. Nowadays, Oshima is famous for being one of the places that residents of Tokyo go to surf, but the island still has groups of dancers who perform to traditional songs from the island.

Leaving behind the views of Oshima, we make our way on foot along the cliffs of Jogasaki until we arrive at the Kadowaki lighthouse. We climb the stairs right to the top of the lighthouse. The views are breathtaking. We can see splendid columns of basalt rising from the sea so vertically they don't look real. They seem to defy the sea's powers of erosion. Geologically speaking, the coastline of the Izu peninsula is young. In fact, only a few miles away is the Mount Omuro volcano, which I climbed on another of my trips to Izu.

Beyond the lighthouse is the Kadowakitsuri Suspension Bridge. The wind is so strong that it makes the bridge sway and crossing it makes us feel dizzy. On the other side of the bridge we can see groups of young people climbing up the basalt rocks and throwing acrobatic poses, taking photos on their phones to upload to social media. We finish our morning by eating a bento under the pines with views of the suspension bridge.

We spend several more days exploring the peninsula, leaving early in the morning and coming back each evening to our base, the house with views of the sea from the terrace and the Odoriko train line behind.

On our last day at the house in Izu, the sakura tree in the garden begins to bloom and when we get back to Tokyo the parks are covered in beautiful cherry blossom.

Kusatsu Onsen

I went to make myself a green tea in the kitchen we have at the office. As the tea brewed I looked out of the window at Mount Fuji, bathed in the red light of the sunset. Shimizu came into the kitchen and without saying a word, stood next to me and started to take photos of the legendary mountain.

"My parents are coming to Japan soon. Recommend me a special place for a trip; they already know the usual stuff," I said to him.

Shimizu stopped taking photos but stayed lost in thought, staring at the mountains on the horizon. Several seconds passed in silence; if I hadn't known him for years I'd have thought he was ignoring me. Shimizu is one of those people who's in no hurry to speak, always taking to time to think before opening his mouth.

"Have you ever been to Kusatsu?" he replied finally. "It's one of the *onsen* with the best hot-spring waters in Japan."

Just a few weeks after having this conversation I was driving around snow-covered mountains

looking for the legendary waters of Kusatsu.

Kusatsu is a town in Gunma Prefecture famous for its hot springs with many curative properties. It has fewer than ten thousand inhabitants, and you can get almost anywhere on foot. It is regarded as one of the three most important hot spring areas of Japan, together with Gero Onsen and Arima Onsen. In the municipal area of Kusatsu 8,400 gallons (32,000 liters) of water per minute come to the surface, making it the most active onsen in Japan.

The waters of Kusatsu cure all ailments except those brought on by love.
Even when it rains you won't get wet
— *popular Kusatsu saying.*

How to Get There

There are no direct trains to Kusatsu. We went by car, but you can also go by bus from the railway station at Naganohara Kusatsuguchi (長野原草津口), which takes twenty-five minutes. It's possible to visit as a day trip from Tokyo, but ideally you should stay overnight in one of the town's hotels or ryokan.

The emblem of Kusatsu is the cascade of volcanic water right in the center of town.

The Underworld of Sai No Kawara

The deity Jizo became popular in the Heian period (794–1185). During this era the principles of Pure Land Buddhism began to spread in Japan, along with the concept of the possibility of going to hell after death. The deity Jizo promised to free those who were trapped in hell, especially children.

One of those responsible for spreading the fear of going to hell was the monk Genshin (942–1017) who wrote a book entitled *Ojoyoshu* (The essentials of salvation) in which he described the cycle of death and rebirth.

The book also tells the legend of the children of Sai no Kawara. According to this legend, children who die prematurely are sent to the underworld as punishment for causing pain and suffering to their parents.

Sai no Kawara is the name of the bank of the river that flows from life to the afterlife, through a kind of underworld limbo. The dead children waiting in this limbo pile up stones on the river bank in the hope of making a

mountain that they can climb to escape and go to heaven.

From time to time, demons from hell, armed with sticks, walk along the river bank destroying the towers of stones and frightening the children.

Jizo goes down to the river to help the children, hiding them in the sleeves of his clothes. Statues of Jizo are among the most widely seen Buddhist symbols around Japan.

At Kusatsu you can visit the symbolic version of the Sai no Kawara underworld at the Sai no Kawara Park. This park is also an *onsen* hot spring, where you can bathe in the waters of hell.

These are photos of Sai no Kawara, the onsen of hell. Can you find piles of stones? And demons with sticks?

In Sai no Kawara, water comes straight from the ground to form green pools. No vegetation will grow in these sulfurous conditions.

Legend has it that the hot springs of Kusatsu were discovered two thousand years ago by Yamato Takeru, son of Emperor Keiko, the twelfth emperor of Japan. He is said to have come across the hot springs when he got lost following the flight of an eagle in the mountains.

However, the first appearance of Kusatsu in historical records was in 1595, in correspondence between shogun Tokugawa Ieyasu and samurai Toyotomi Hideyoshi. In one of the messages, Toyotomi Hideyoshi advises Tokugawa Ieyasu to go to Kusatsu to bathe in the thermal springs, telling him that they'll cure any complaint that he might be suffering from.

Tokugawa wasn't able to go in person to Kusatsu but he ordered his servants to travel there and bring the miraculous water to his castle.

Later, during the Edo period (1603–1868), the popularity of Kusatsu grew as syphilis and gonorrhea started to spread in Tokyo. A belief circulating at the time was that one of the best ways to cure or relieve the pain of both venereal diseases was to bathe in the volcanic waters of Kusatsu.

The waters of Kusatsu are considered to be acidic, hence the belief that they are good for killing all types of microbes. They say that if you throw a one yen coin into the waters of Kusatsu, a week later it will have disappeared, having been completely corroded. If you bathe in the Kusatsu water, don't wear any kind of metal jewelry.

Subterranean water comes to the surface at more than a hundred points in the town. These hot springs are put to use by hotels, public onsen and ryokan. About 90 percent of the town's economy revolves around the exploitation of its waters.

Once you've arrived in Kusatsu, if you want to find the town center, all you need is your sense

ABOVE *Ashinoyu* are foot baths, where people can sit for a while and soak their feet in hot-spring water. RIGHT Izanagi and Izanami creating the first island of Japan with the *amanobuko* spear.

of smell to guide you. In the town square there's a great pool of steaming volcanic water called Yubatake, which reeks overpoweringly of hydrogen sulfide.

Yubatake is the town's main spring, from which more than a thousand gallons (four thousand liters) of water pour every minute. All the water is channeled by a system of wooden piping which allows it to fall in a cascade on the other side of the square. A type of salt called *yunohana* (hot water sediment) accumulates in the pipes.

In most of the springs in Kusatsu Onsen the water is too hot to bathe in when it comes out of the ground and needs to be cooled. One of the methods used to bring down the temperature of the water is to stir it with wooden boards. This technique, known as *yumomi,* developed into a dance or ritual which is now one of the town's tourist attractions. Keep an eye out for public dance performances where you'll be able to see how the water is cooled using the famous boards, and maybe even have a go yourself!

Ise Grand Shrine

The Ise Grand Shrine, in Ise, Mie Prefecture, is regarded as Japan's most important Shinto shrine. In this section, I'll take at look at its historical and modern-day significance.

According to Japanese mythology, thousands of years ago the universe consisted of silence, darkness and a mass of shapeless matter.

At a certain moment, particles within the shapeless matter began to move and collide with each other, creating the first sounds. These movements created the clouds and the sky, where the first three gods of Japanese mythology spontaneously appeared. They are called Amenominakanushi, Takamimusubi and Kamimusubi. Beneath them was a sphere formed of disorganized particles that the three gods decided to call Earth. Several generations of gods later, the goddess Izanami and the god Izanagi, the creators of Japan, were born.

Izanami and Izanagi were commanded to descend to Earth to put it in order. They accepted the responsibility and were given a sacred spear called *amanobuko* 天沼矛 (lit., spear of the sky and the sea) that would help them fulfil their mission. They traveled together until they came to a floating bridge close to Earth. They leaned over the rail and stirred the waters of the sea with the amanobuko spear. When they took the spear from the water, the drops of salt water on the tip condensed to create the first island of Japan, called Awajishima 淡路島.

Using the same spear they continued their work of creation, bringing forth Honshu, Shikoku, Kyushu and the rest of the islands that make up the Japanese archipelago.

They also created forests, mountains and rivers. When they had finished their arduous task, Izanami and Izanagi built a house in Awajishima and got married. To conclude the job they had been entrusted with, they had lots of children who would continue to care for Japan, including Amaterasu, the sun goddess, regarded as the "mother" of Japan.

According to legend, Jinmu, the great-grandson of Amaterasu, born more than 2,700 years ago, was the first emperor of Japan, and was believed to be the first human with the blood of the gods. Naruhito, the current emperor of Japan, is thought by many to be a direct descendant of Jinmu.

Just over 2,000 years ago, Suinin, the eleventh Emperor of Japan entrusted his daughter Yamatohime with the mission of finding a permanent location for the worship of Amaterasu. The legend says that Yamatohime had spent twenty years traveling around Japan unable to find a suitable place, when she heard the voice of Amaterasu as she was walking along the banks of a river running through the forests of Ise.

Amaterasu expressed to Yamatohime her desire to live next to the flowing water of the river, feeling the protection of the trees and contemplating the immensity of the sea. Her wish was granted and in her honor Ise Grand Shrine was built there.

Since then, the shrine has been rebuilt every twenty years on the very spot chosen by Yamatohime. The original plans are followed and the same type of Japanese cypress is used for construction.

人間宣言
The Humanity Declaration

When the Second World War ended, one of the conditions imposed on Japan by the United States was that Emperor Hirohito must lose his divine status. Until that point, the emperor of Japan was regarded by the Japanese constitution as a direct descendant of Amaterasu, the goddess who created Japan.

Arahitogami 現人神 (lit., now, person, god) means "god in human form." Emperor Hirohito was an arahitogami until 1946, when he was obliged by Douglas MacArthur to sign a document called the *Ningen Sengen* 人間宣言, known in English as the Humanity Declaration. In other words, in signing the ningen sengen, Emperor Hirohito renounced his status as arahitogami and admitted to being an ordinary human being.

These are the words of the original document which is kept in the National Diet Library:

朕ト爾等國民トノ間ノ紐帯ハ、終始相互ノ信頼ト敬愛トニ依リテ結バレ、單ナル神話ト傳説トニ依リテ生ゼルモノニ非ズ。天皇ヲ以テ現御神トシ、且日本國民ヲ以テ他ノ民族ニ優越セル民族ニシテ、延テ世界ヲ支配スベキ運命ヲ有ストノ架空ナル觀念ニ基クモノニモ非ズ。

"The ties between us and our people have always been based on mutual trust and affection. They do not depend upon mere legends and myths. They are not predicated on the false conception that the emperor is divine, and that the Japanese people are superior to other races and fated to rule the world."

One issue with the Humanity Declaration is that despite Hirohito's renunciation of his divine status, at no time does he deny that he is a direct descendant of Amaterasu. Consequently the Emperor stopped being a god, but didn't stop being a descendant of the gods.

One of the problems is that in the document the word *akitsumikami* 現御神 (lit., now, honorable, god) is used instead of *arahitogami* 現人神 (lit., now, person, god). Notice that only the central character of the word has changed, but according to linguistic purists the meaning is different: the first form means something closer to "embodiment of god" and the second means "god in human form."

Some say it's possible to lose the status of "embodiment of god" without losing the status of "god in human form." Therefore on signing the document, Hirohito would have renounced his status as akitsumikami but not his status as arahitogami.

These ambiguities have created a lot of confusion. Many Japanese still believe the current emperor is a god and that all Japanese people are descendants of Amaterasu. They argue that a signature on a piece of paper does not have the power to do away with the divine status of a *kami* or god.

Note: I use the word god as a synonym of kami.

No nails or metal components of any sort are used, only wood.

According to Shinto, nature dies and is born constantly, and everything is impermanent. The tradition of rebuilding the shrine maintains the freshness and the purity of the place. The aim of the cycle of rebuilding is that the shrine is at once old, original, pure and new. The shrine was last rebuilt in 2013, according to the original plans and following the tradition that began when Yamato-hime heard the voice of Amaterasu while walking through the area two thousand years ago.

Ise Grand Shrine in the Postwar Period

In the early 1940s in the United States, hundreds of scientists were working on the Manhattan Project, an experiment with the particles and fundamental forces which make up the universe. But the final creations of this group of scientists were not islands, rivers, lakes, forests or mountains: they were Little Boy and Fat Man, two atomic bombs, whose energy ended the lives of hundreds of thousands of people, reduced two cities to ash and put an end to Japan's imperialist ambitions. Indirectly they also put an end to the divine status of the Emperor, the supposed direct descendant of Amaterasu, the sun goddess. At the end of the Second World War, Emperor Hirohito renounced his divine status on signing the Humanity Declaration before the US general Douglas MacArthur.

The Manhattan Project ended the divine lineage of Japanese emperors. Hirohito was officially the last Japanese god. It is said that all the Japanese gods, including Hirohito, meet every October at Ise Grand Shrine.

July 2011

We cycled as far as the *torii* gate inviting us to enter the sacred territory of the Ise Grand Shrine. We crossed Uji Bridge and went into a forest, where we walked under the gaze of the trees, each one of which is said to be home to a *kami*. We stopped to rest for a while next to the river, home of the river god, and then we strolled around the wooden structures of the shrine, whose columns emerge straight from the gravel-covered ground. We marveled at the way the wood of the shrine buildings blends with the natural wood of the forest that surrounds them, making it difficult to distinguish the natural from the man-made.

At the far end of one of the path we glimpsed the inner part of the shrine, known as Kotai Jingu. This is the home of Amaterasu, and is considered the holiest place in Japan. Our view was obscured by a white sheet marking the limit beyond which we humans were not allowed to go. We could only see Kotai Jingu when the sheet moved in the breeze.

A few months later, in October, thousands of

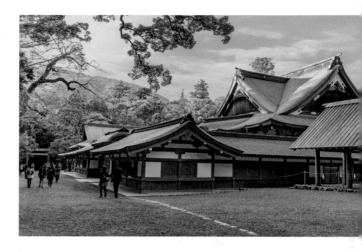

kami (gods) gathered at the Ise Grand Shrine, as they do every year. Also attending the meeting was Naruhito, Emperor of Japan, who though he isn't yet officially a *kami*, according to Japanese mythology is descended from them.

I like to think that when the meeting was over, many of the kami went off together to the *onsen* hot springs that featured in *Spirited Away*, to enjoy bathing and relaxing.

Notes from My Travel Diary

When we stopped to rest next to the Ise River I remembered the moment when Haku, the river god in *Spirited Away*, remembers his real name:

Haku Thanks, Chihiro. My real name is Nigihayami Kohaku Nushi.

Chihiro Nigihayami?

Haku Nigihayami Kohaku Nushi.

Chihiro What a beautiful name. It sounds like the name of a kami.

Haku I remember too, how you fell into me as a child. You had dropped your shoe.

Chihiro Yes, you carried me to shallow water, Kohaku.

[They put their faces together, close enough to kiss.]

Chihiro I'm so grateful!

Meoto Iwa, the Wedded Rocks

After creating the first Japanese island with a drop of water from the *amanobuko* sacred spear, Izanagi and Izanami came down from the heavens and built a column which they called *Amenomihashira* (the pillar of the sky). In a kind of marriage ceremony they walked around the column in opposite directions and when they met, Izanami said to Izanagi: "You are so beautiful, kind and young," to which Izanagi replied: "Oh, you are the youngest and the most beautiful." Without another word they made love for the first time next to the Amenomihashira column, and a little later Hiroku, their first son, was born. He was born disfigured, and they decided to get rid of him by putting him inside a canoe and letting the ocean current carry him away. Hiroku didn't die; his strength of spirit allowed him to survive. (In time he came to be known as Ebisu, the god of good fortune and of fishermen.)

Displeased, Izanagi and Izanami returned to heaven to ask the gods what they had done wrong. Their superiors told them: "You made a mistake when you walked around the Amenomihashira; when you meet, the male must speak first."

They tried again, walking around the Amenomihashira column in opposite directions until they met, but this time it was Izanagi, who spoke first. As their marriage ceremony had been conducted according to the rules, they went on to have many children who would be responsible for carrying on with the task of creation.

2020 Years Ago

Yamatohime, daughter of the emperor of Japan, had spent years searching for the perfect location to build a temple dedicated to the sun goddess Amaterasu, one of the daughters of Izanagi and Izanami, conceived next to the column of Amenomihashira. Legend has it that it was Yamatohime that found the location of the Ise Grand Shrine (see page 175).

In another legend, Yamatohime was walking along a beach in present-day Mie Prefecture. On the horizon she could make out two rocks rising from the water like the shoulders of a god. The pair of rocks left her so spellbound that she came back twice to appreciate their beauty. A story grew up that the two beautiful rocks weren't the shoulders of a god, they were Izanagi and Izanami.

1,500 Years Ago

The legend of the two rocks that were Izanagi and Izanami was passed down through generations of Japanese. About 1,500 years ago a group of monks decided it was necessary to tie together, unite and marry the Izanagi and Izanami rocks using a *shimenawa* rope, which is a symbol of union in Japanese culture.

Enmusubi 縁結び is one of the many words in the Japanese language that mean "marry." The first character 縁 means "cord" and 結び means "tie or bind." It's interesting that in English we also talk about "marriage ties."

The monks made an enormous shimenawa rope using rice straw and tied the two rocks together with it. At the top of the bigger rock, which represents Izanagi, they placed a wooden *torii* gate.

Ever since, Izanagi and Izanami, who were first married as they circled the Amenomihashira column, have been eternally united. The two rocks joined by the shimenawa rope became known as Meoto Iwa 夫婦岩, where 夫 means "husband," 婦 means "wife" and 岩 means "rock."

Meoto Iwa is visited by thousands of tourists

each year, and is said to bring good fortune in matters of the heart.

July 2011

The dawn light woke us as it gently pierced the shoji paper panels covering the windows in our room. We left the ryokan, the oldest building in the street and one which seemed to come straight out of an Akira Kurosawa movie, and got on our bikes. Our destination was Meoto Iwa.

We pedaled toward the ocean, leaving the town of Ise behind, crossing several rivers and passing green rice fields. The sun blazed down, but the smell of the ocean, which grew stronger and stronger, gave us the energy to keep on pedaling. An hour later came our first glimpse of blue on the horizon, and soon we spotted the first torii gate of Meoto Iwa. We rode along the seashore until we arrived at the gate, got off our bikes and entered the sacred ground. Walking between the sea and the cliffs awakened memories of walks I'd had with my parents along beaches in Spain when I was a child. It also reminded me of Miyajima, another beautiful location in Japan where the ocean and the land merge to create a shrine (see page 165).

We visited Meoto Iwa on a bright summer's morning, but the view of the rocks changes according to the season and the time of day, whether it's under the light of the moon with its power to make the tides rise and fall, whether it's windy with waves crashing, whether it's sunny or cloudy, even the angle at which you stand . . . these can all influence how you see the Wedded Rocks.

People say that one of the best times to see Meoto Iwa in all its glory is at dawn during the months of May, June and July, when the sun is framed between the rocks as it rises. With luck, if the weather's good, you might also make out the distant silhouette of Mount Fuji.

September 2018

The rope which joins the two rocks of Meoto Iwa is changed three times a year: in May, September and December.

On the television news I see several men dressed in white, climbing onto the rocks to change the old *shimenawa* rope for a new one.

Time is too slow for those who wait, too swift for those who fear, too long for those who grieve, too short for those who rejoice, but for those who love, time is eternity.

— William Shakespeare

LEFT The Wedded Rocks framed by the *torii* gate.
ABOVE The two "married" rocks are tied together by an enormous rope made of rice straw.

"*Don't look to follow in the footsteps of the wise, search for what they searched for.*"

—Matsuo Basho

CHAPTER 10

More of My Favorite Things

The office of the first company I worked for in Japan, as an intern, was somewhere in the middle of nowhere between Tokyo and Yokohama, in an area with nothing other than factories, rice fields, love hotels and a few houses. Close by was the Sony factory that Steve Jobs visited when he traveled to Japan for the first time. Apart from this, there was nothing worthy of mention.

To entertain me, my work colleagues were kind enough to take me to several restaurants next to the nearest railway station. I remember one in particular, whose wooden walls and columns made you forget you were in an industrial area. What's more, the waiters and waitresses were dressed as Japanese farmers from the past. They served *monjayaki*, a traditional type of omelet that was delicious. That restaurant made me feel as though I'd been transported by time machine to a singular and special place.

As it was only my first year in Japan, I thought this particular restaurant I went to with my colleagues was unique, and I recommended it to everybody. I didn't yet know that there were tens of thousands of similar restaurants in Japan. They're called izakaya.

Izakaya Restaurants

Having dinner at an izakaya restaurant is so entertaining. Trying all kinds of new culinary delights is part of the fun, but so is the decor and atmosphere of each place.

LEFT Tea ceremony takes place in a simple room with tatami-mat flooring.
RIGHT You don't go to an izakaya for food, but for the atmosphere.

If you're traveling and you want to eat dinner, ask for the nearest izakaya (they are usually closed in the daytime and open only in the evening). They serve all kinds of food and have several types of seating arrangement depending on what you want: private rooms for groups or couples, areas with tatami mats where you can eat sitting on the floor, and areas with Western-style tables. Another feature of izakaya is that they serve alcoholic drinks.

居酒屋 Izakaya

The closest translation of izakaya in English would be "pub" or "bar-restaurant."

The individual characters that make up the word 居酒屋 izakaya have the following meanings:

居 be or rest

酒 alcohol

屋 shop

The quality of food in izakaya ranges from average to good, in some cases even very good. But you don't go to izakaya for the quality of the food, you go for the atmosphere, the decor and the flexibility they offer. They are great places for all kinds of celebrations from birthdays to farewell parties. This is something the Japanese value greatly, because they're reluctant to have parties in their own homes.

The decor of some izakaya will make you feel as though you've traveled in a time machine back to the Edo period. Others might transport you to the future. The care the Japanese take with the inte-rior design of any restaurant is extraordinary. For me the best thing about izakaya is that it's a kind of holistic experience, from the moment you go in until the moment you leave. An izakaya can transport you to another dimension, and you can forget for a while that you're in the center of Tokyo or in a village in the middle of the countryside.

I love going for dinner in an izakaya; they have such a relaxing effect on me. The effect is especially powerful when you've been walking around Shibuya surrounded by thousands of people, skyscrapers, neon signs, and giant advertising screens, and then you step inside a building and take an elevator to the tenth floor. You push open an old wooden door and inside it's all dark wood and tatami mats. You take off your shoes and a waiter leads you to a private room where you sit on the floor at a low table.

This capacity to create exceptional spaces sometimes extends to entire streets or even neighborhoods. For example, Ridley Scott was inspired by the atmosphere of the entertainment district of Dotonbori in Osaka to create the first *Blade Runner* movie in 1982.

In Tokyo there are fewer and fewer areas specializing in traditional restaurants. One of the best ways of knowing that you're getting close to one of these areas is to look out for *chochin* oblong paper lanterns hanging from doorways. My favorite areas for traditional izakaya are in Shinjuku, near the east exit of the station; under the railway tracks in Shinbashi; Kagurazaka; and around Senso-ji temple in Asakusa.

Shiitake Mushrooms

Shiitake mushrooms are widely used in Japanese cuisine. They're one of the ingredients I nearly always buy when I go to the supermarket because they go well with virtually everything.

They're rich in vitamin D, and the best thing is you can find shiitake all year round thanks to the fact that it's a species cultivated relatively easily in greenhouses.

If you go to a *yakitori, yakiniku* or izakaya restaurant, they'll almost certainly have them on the menu or you can order them by saying *"Shiitake onegaishimasu* (椎茸お願いします)."

Senko Hanabi Fireworks

Senko hanabi 線香花火, whose literal translation is "incense stick fireworks," are small fireworks that you can buy in convenience stores in summer. It's traditional to enjoy them on beaches and in parks on warm nights.

It is said that watching senko hanabi sparkling in the darkness can help us forget about the past and the future, luring our consciousness into the present and making us fall into the hypnotic state of *mono no aware,* when we realize how beautiful and yet how short our lives are.

Senko hanabi help to awaken our connection the hypnotic state mono no aware, *which reminds us that life is at once beautiful and short.*

Hasedera Temple in Kamakura

Legend says that in the year 711 a monk named Tokudo had a pair of statues of the "goddess" Kannon sculpted. (I put the word goddess in quotation marks because in fact Kannon is a bodhisattva, with eleven heads.)

One of the two statues was sent to Hasedera temple in Nara and the other was placed on a boat floating on the sea near Kamakura to help bring good fortune to the locals. Years later a storm swept the boat onto the beach.

A nobleman of the Fujiwara family found the statue in the sand and restored it. He took it to a hillside in Kamakura where he decided to establish another temple named Hasedera 長谷寺 in which to house the rescued statue.

FACING PAGE Grilled shiitake being prepared at an izakaya.
LEFT The small hand-held fireworks known as *senko hanabi* are a feature of summer evenings in Japan.

Hasedera temple still exists today and one of the best times to visit is at the end of spring when the hillsides are covered with *ajisai*, lilac-colored hydrangeas.

At the temple entrance there's a landscaped area with ponds and lotus flowers and a set of stairs alongside which are hundreds of statues of Jizo, the guardian deity of children.

At the top of the stairs are the two main buildings of the temple: the *Kannon-do* (main hall) and the *Amida-do* (secondary hall). In the Kannon-do is the statue of Kannon with the eleven heads. In the Amida-do there's a ten-foot (three-meter) high statue of an Amida Buddha. The Amida Buddhas are highly venerated objects in the Jodo Buddhist sect. This statue was sculpted by Minamoto no Yoritomo (1147–1199), who was the founder of the Kamakura shogunate.

A typical way to round off a visit to Hasedera is to enjoy the views of Sagami Bay. From a viewpoint in the temple grounds you can see the beaches at Yuigahama and Zaimokuza, where many bloody battles were fought in feudal times. On the horizon you can see the town of Zushi, and at the end of Yuigahama Beach is Ominesan cape, protruding into the waters where Kannon floated for years until she was rescued.

MY TRAVEL TRIPS
Visiting Kamakura

The temple of Hasedera is near the exit of Hase Station in Kamakura. Also worth a visit is the Great Buddha of Kamakura at Kotoku-in temple, a few minutes' walk from Hasedera, heading away from the sea.

ABOVE **The Great Buddha of Kamakura.**

Stunning crimson foliage at Hasedera temple in fall.

BELOW and RIGHT The different types of Jizo statue at Hasedera temple include the very popular smiling trio below.

Jizo Deities

Jizo is one of the Buddhist deities who enjoys great popularity in Japan. As well as protecting travelers, Jizo looks after the weak, and children especially; this deity is the savior of children who die before or during birth. Families who have lost a child in this way can go to a temple and offer to add a Jizo statue. Each one of the little statues that you'll inevitably come across as you are traveling around Japan represents one of these children. Sometimes Jizo states are hidden in the vegetation near temples and other times you come across them in dark forest areas. You also find them watching over you by the roadside; these are the Jizo that protect travelers.

There are many types of Jizo; some smile and some don't. The majority wait patiently at the entrance to graveyards and usually wear a crocheted hat to ward off the cold, and a red bib so they don't get hungry. Parents are responsible for changing the bibs and the hats of the Jizo statues. In this way, they are asking the Jizo to help the child that never arrived to escape from the Buddhist limbo of Sai no Kawara (see page 173).

I will never be a Buddha until I empty every hell and save every being. — Jizo

In Kamakura, a monk rings his bell and chants.

Hiking in Japan

If you only visit the megacities of Tokyo, Yokohama, Osaka, Kyoto and Hiroshima, your view of the country will be limited to urban Japan. But almost 90 percent of Japan consists of countryside, most of it made up of mountains. This is a fact that is easy to forget when you're spending your days in one of the big cities.

In 1964, a mountaineer called Kyuya Fukada published a book entitled *One Hundred Mountains of Japan*, a reference guide that is widely used by mountaineering enthusiasts in Japan. The book became even more famous when Emperor Naruhito bought it, when he was still Crown Prince. He used it to "get away" from the Imperial Palace and go mountain climbing. It is reported that one of his dreams is to reach the summits of all one hundred mountains listed in the book.

Mountains are the most characteristic topographical feature of Japan. The majority are covered in forest. Many of them are volcanos, both active and dormant, and as such are rockier and more inhospitable.

Japan's four distinct seasons bring changes in the natural scenery that can add to your pleasure. If you visit the mountains of Nikko, north of Tokyo, in summer, the landscape will be nothing like the Nikko you can enjoy at the time of *koyo* (autumn leaves), when everything is tinged gold and red, heralding the arrival of the cold weather.

Adding a touch of nature to your trip to Japan is easy; there are hiking routes practically everywhere you go. These routes cater for all levels; if you have no experience of climbing mountains it's best to choose the easier options. In Japan there are really dangerous mountains that are not recommended unless you're experienced. Close to Tokyo the most popular trail is the one on Mount Takao, the summit of which is 1,965 feet (599 meters) above sea level. You can reach Takao Station in about fifty minutes from Shinjuku, on the Chuo Line.

My Mitake Mountaineering Diary

We set off to climb Mount Mitake, to the west of Tokyo. At the beginning of the trail we came across a group of elderly people doing stretching exercises before starting their hike. It is always interesting to see the serious attention that the Japanese pay to detail, whatever they are doing.

Our group, all in our thirties and forties, didn't take things so seriously. We strolled along enjoying the scenery, stopping now and then to take photos. We stopped to relax and eat a few sandwiches next to a waterfall.

At first we kept ahead of the old people; we had energy to spare. But after a couple of hours we began to tire and they overtook us. They even tried to egg us on when they saw the defeat in our faces. Finally we reached the top, though it took us longer than them.

Lesson learned: if you see a group of pensioners doing stretches at the start of a hiking trail, the walk ahead might be more difficult than you think.

How to get to Mitake
To get to Mount Mitake, take the Chuo Line from Shinjuku Station to Tachikawa. At Tachikawa change to the Ome Line and go to Mitake Station. From there you get the bus to the cable car, and that's where the adventure begins.

On the route to the top of Mount Mitake we came across elderly people exercising, and shrines with spectacular views.

Akihabara Radio Center

Radio Center ラジオセンター (*rajio senta*) is a shopping mall specializing in electrical component stores in Tokyo's Akihabara district. It's a little corner that has survived the passage of time; here you can find anything from the latest FPGAs to vacuum tubes. You'll find stores that specialize in multimeters, transistors, condensers, robot components, photoelectric cells, LEDs . . . the list is endless. What I like most about Radio Center is the cyberpunk atmosphere you breathe as you walk through its narrow corridors crammed with cables. It reminds me of the market for junk and mechanical-electrical parts in the manga *Gunnm, Battle Angel Alita*.

If you love building electrical circuits or you're mad about robotics, this is paradise. If you're not interested in electronics, a stroll through this mall is still one of the most interesting experiences you can have in Akihabara: watching businessmen in suits and ties rummaging through filthy cardboard boxes for vacuum tubes is priceless.

Radio Center used to be the name of an entire district of Akihabara where electrical equipment began to be sold in the fifties. What they mostly sold were radios, hence the name. Then came TVs in the seventies, computers in the eighties, and since the nineties Akihabara has been devoted to hobbies in general: electronics, manga, anime, etc. Gradually the district has become a mecca for freaks and otaku from all over the world.

A multitude of stores and shopping malls opened and closed as the neighborhood went through each successive cycle of transformation, but Radio Center has survived these changes for more than fifty years.

In Akihabara you can appreciate the Japanese philosophy of looking after the past and creating the future. You can buy the most up-to-date game consoles and electrical equipment, but you can also haggle with the shopkeeper over the prices of Commodore 64 games or an original Walkman.

> Getting there: the Radio Center has two entrances; one is right next to the Akihabara Electric Town exit of Akihabara Station, and the other entrance is at the point where the train tracks cross the street.

The narrow passageways of the Radio Center are a riot of electronic components.

Shisa Lion-Dogs

Shisa are types of mythological figures in the shape of lion-dogs. They are usually found in doorways or on the roofs of buildings, or in parks and temple grounds. They originate from Okinawa, where they are believed to have the power to protect against evil spirits.

Legend has it that a Chinese diplomat came to visit the king of Ryukyu (present-day Okinawa) and stayed at Shuri Castle. As a gift for the king he brought a necklace with a little figure of a lion-dog. The king of Ryukyu liked it so much that from then on he always wore it.

According to local legend, not far from the king's castle there was a coastal village whose inhabitants had long been living in fear of a gigantic sea dragon that was eating their children and destroying their houses. One day the king visited the village, stood in front of the dragon and raised the little figure of the shisa on his necklace, causing a huge rock to fall from the sky that crushed the wicked dragon's tail, leaving it paralyzed forever.

Like may things that come from Okinawa in Japan's far south, shisa have an obvious Chinese influence. They always make me think of the lions in the Forbidden City in Beijing. But even if you've never visited China, you'll probably have seen these lion-dog statues at the entrances to Asian restaurants in the West, where they are commonly used as decorations.

There are two versions of shisa: the male, with its mouth open, and the female, with its mouth closed. In the Tsuboya neighborhood of Naha, Okinawa's capital city, five minutes' walk south from Kokusai-dori Avenue, you may be able to see traditional craftspeople at work creating these magical creatures.

Shisa are mythological figures in the form of lion-dogs that can be seen in many places in Japan.

Green Tea

When I first arrived in Japan fifteen years ago, one of the first things I noticed was the number of people drinking bottled green tea. Immediately my curiosity took me in the direction of a drink machine in Shibuya and instead of buying a fizzy drink, I pressed the button for one of the green teas. I was expecting a cold, sweet tea. Imagine my shock when I took my first mouthful to find it was exceptionally bitter and completely unsweetened – yuck!

Some years later, after drinking a lot of green tea and learning to appreciate its flavor, I was in San Francisco and I happened to order a tea with lemon and sugar. I took a sip – yuck! I felt as if I was drinking sugared water. That's how I became a fan of green tea without sugar.

While tea ceremony (above) is a traditional way of enjoying green tea, you can buy bottled green tea from any Japanese drink machine.

In Chinese and in Japanese, the character 茶 is used to signify tea. In Japanese it's pronounced *cha*. To refer to green tea they use the word *ocha* お茶.

Green teas can be classified in many ways, but the main factors are: the time of year the tea was harvested; the way the leaves are dried; the length of time the leaves have been exposed to the sun.

Sencha 煎茶 is the type of green tea most widely consumed in Japan. If the leaves are from the first harvest (April and May) it's called *shincha* (a lighter shade of green), and if it's the summer harvest it's called *bancha*. A type of bancha that is quite popular is *hojicha* ほうじ茶, made by roasting the leaves and stems. Hojicha is one of the gentlest green teas and is usually served at midday to accompany lunch. If you're given complimentary tea when you go into a restaurant in Japan, it's usually hojicha. It has a light brown color and is good served either hot, or cold over ice.

Gyokuro 玉露 is a high-quality tea and is considerably more expensive than sencha. During the last few weeks before harvesting, the plants are covered to keep them out of the sunlight; this increases the quantity of theanine and caffeine in the leaves. Gyokuro is darker in color than sencha.

Matcha 抹茶 is powdered green tea that is dissolved in hot water. This is the tea used in the tea ceremony. It has a more intense green color and a more bitter flavor than sencha and gyokuro. Some people can't stand its strong taste, but I love it. Matcha is often used to flavor candy, ice cream, cupcakes and desserts in general.

Matcha is prepared by stirring the powder with a *chasen*, a kind of brush made from bamboo cane, in a *chawan* bowl until a fine layer of foam forms. Matcha can be served cold or hot depending on the season, and is usually accompanied by something sweet.

Uloncha 烏龍茶 is a type of Chinese tea with less caffeine than green tea. Drunk cold during the heat of summer, it's very refreshing. If you're out in the evening and don't want to drink alcohol, uloncha is a good drink to order as its low caffeine content won't keep you awake when you go to bed.

Mugicha 麦茶 is made exclusively from barley, and as such has no caffeine. It has a yellowish color.

Genmaicha 玄米茶 is another cereal-based tea, made from a mixture of toasted rice and green tea leaves. Like mugicha, it has a yellowish color.

Matcha is bright green and has a strong, bitter flavor. It's usually accompanied by something sweet, occasionally by something savory.

Published by Tuttle Publishing, an imprint of Periplus Editions (HK) Ltd

www.tuttlepublishing.com

ISBN 978-4-8053-1652-8

Distributed by

North America, Latin America & Europe
Tuttle Publishing
364 Innovation Drive, North Clarendon,VT 05759-9436 USA
Tel: 1 (802) 773-8930; Fax: 1 (802) 773-6993
info@tuttlepublishing.com; www.tuttlepublishing.com

Japan
Tuttle Publishing
Yaekari Building, 3rd Floor, 5-4-12 Osaki
Shinagawa-ku, Tokyo 141-0032
Tel: (81) 3 5437-0171; Fax: (81) 3 5437-0755
sales@tuttle.co.jp; www.tuttle.co.jp

Asia Pacific
Berkeley Books Pte Ltd
3 Kallang Sector #04-01, Singapore 349278
Tel: (65) 67412178; Fax: (65) 67412179
inquiries@periplus.com.sg; www.tuttlepublishing.com

24 23 22   6 5 4 3 2

Printed in Singapore   2201TP

Photo Credits

All photos by Hector Garcia except the following:
Shutterstock: p18 top; p21 bottom; p23; p86 top left; p96; p114; p121, bottom; p134; p142; p157 bottom right; p158 top; p159 all; p162; p164–165 all; p167–169 all; p177–178 all; p183 right; p184 all; p190 top; p191 top.
Wikimedia Commons: p28–29; p31; p38; p74; p76; p80–81; p149; p176.
Models in pictures: Yurie Shimizu, Mayuko Hirono, Carlos Donderis, Alejandro Cremades, Gami Satoko and Yoshiko Fujimura.

"BOOKS TO SPAN THE EAST AND WEST"

Tuttle Publishing was founded in 1832 in the small New England town of Rutland, Vermont [USA]. Our core values remain as strong today as they were then—to publish best-in-class books which bring people together one page at a time. In 1948, we established a publishing office in Japan—and Tuttle is now a leader in publishing English-language books about the arts, languages and cultures of Asia. The world has become a much smaller place today and Asia's economic and cultural influence has grown. Yet the need for meaningful dialogue and information about this diverse region has never been greater. Over the past seven decades, Tuttle has published thousands of books on subjects ranging from martial arts and paper crafts to language learning and literature—and our talented authors, illustrators, designers and photographers have won many prestigious awards. We welcome you to explore the wealth of information available on Asia at **tuttlepublishing.com.**